DOOMSDAY
THE SURVIVOR'S GUIDE

DOOMSDAY
THE SURVIVOR'S GUIDE

David John Lee

HarperCollinsPublishers

HarperCollins*Publishers*
77–85 Fulham Palace Road, London W6 8JB

First published in Great Britain in 1999
by HarperCollins*Publishers*

1 3 5 7 9 10 8 6 4 2

Text Copyright © 1999 David John Lee

David John Lee asserts the moral
right to be identified as the author of this work

A catalogue record for this book is
available from the British Library

ISBN 000 274039 7

Printed and bound in Great Britain by
Caledonian International Book Manufacturing Ltd, Glasgow

CONDITIONS OF SALE
This book is sold subject to the condition that it shall not, by way of trade or otherwise, be lent, re-sold, hired out or otherwise circulated without the publisher's prior consent in any form of binding or cover other than that in which it is published and without a similar condition including this condition being imposed on the subsequent purchaser.

All rights reserved. No part of this publication may be reproduced, stored in a retrieval system, or transmitted, in any form or by any means, electronic, mechanical, photocopying, recording or otherwise, without the prior permission of the publishers.

For my father

CONTENTS

Acknowledgements ix
Introduction x

1 **Ten to One on 11 August (maybe)**
   Mr Matthew Dumbrell awaits the end (with his friend Ron the Holy Spirit)   1

2 **Horrible Things about to Happen**
   What's really going to happen when the sky falls? Armageddon – and how to make sure you're not there   8

3 **Dates: a Course in Doom-Monger Maths**
   Foolproof-ish ways of calculating the final day, with examples – keep tabs with the Rapturometer   22

4 **Slouching to Bethlehem (the Forensic Case)**
   A leading psychologist shows you how to recognize Ultimate Evil using offender profiling – plus pictures   39

5 **Are You the Future Evil World Dictator?**
   Today's hot contenders for the title (including Barney the dinosaur) – the try-it-yourself Triple Six Test   49

6 **What to Wear at the Last Judgement**
   How to meet your Maker and come out smiling (with a little help from *Cosmopolitan* and London's leading image consultants)   66

7 **Aliens are a-Comin'...**
   Will Doomsday come courtesy of the little green men from Alpha Centuri? Top ufologists reveal whether life under the Martians will be heaven or hell   76

8   **Doomsday – the Ad (How to Sell the End of the World)**
    Fed up with that sandwich board? Saatchi & Saatchi give their hot tips on selling Doomsday – fully illustrated   90

9   **Get the Egg off your Face**
    Do failed prophets become social workers? A quasi-Jungian analysis of post-prediction stress disorder   103

10 **Snack-sized Armageddons**
    Our chances of going down the tubes without the help of divine judgement – Patrick Moore and Simon Hughes MP assist   121

11 **And Then...?**
    Does Doomsday tell us anything useful? Thoughts on sex, death and destiny from People Who Should Know What They're Talking About   137

    Appendix I – Revelation: the Summary   148

    Appendix II – The All-time Funniest Gag   152

    Notes   154

ACKNOWLEDGEMENTS

The sources
Very many thanks to all those whose assistance made this book possible. They deserve much credit and bear no blame. In alphabetical order: Marilyn Agee; Professor Richard Bauckham; Jesus, a.k.a. Rev. J. C. 'Steve' Bevilacqua, Business Manager for the Church of the SubGenius; Graham Birdsall, Editor of *UFO Magazine*; Dr Ann Casement; James Catford; Steve Chalke of Oasis Media; Richard Chartres, the Bishop of London; Harry Coney of INFORM at the London School of Economics; Barry Cox of Grey; Matthew Dumbrell (and Ron); George Egg, the greatest stand-up comic since Plato; Paul Gillies, press officer on behalf of Jehovah's Witnesses; Dr Maurice Greenberg; Dr Paul Heelas; Simon Hughes MP; Richard Keeling of Amlin; my neighbour Stephen Lau; Patrick Moore; *Cosmopolitan*'s Mandi Norwood; John Pearce of the Article Numbers Association; Professor David Perrett; Lorna Russell, editor of *Sybil*; Professor Andrew Samuels; Graham Sharpe of William Hill; Angela Slack; Mary Spillane of Color Me Beautiful; prophecy pack rat Todd Strandberg; Michael Willmott, Director of the Future Foundation; and Professor Peter Worsley.

The advertisers
Particular thanks to Fish, Jill Simpson and Dave Askwith at Saatchi & Saatchi, who gave their company motto its ultimate test by running a campaign for God. They each get a weekend break for two in the Heavenly City, plus vouchers. Pictures of the Saatchi & Saatchi campaign appear in Chapter 8.

Doomsday campaigns put together by other leading UK advertising agencies are distributed throughout the book. It isn't often that creatives are asked to produce the goods *and* write the brief. Some brilliant stuff came out, and if God ever ends the world in earnest, I'm sure they'll all get the job. Heartfelt thanks to:

Paul Young and Ben Kay (Abbott Mead Vickers), Rosie Elston, Mary-Sue Lawrence and Lieve Cornil (Mustoe Merriman Herring Levy) and Tim Lewis (Unreal), David Woods, Peter Harle and Tivy Davies (TBWA GGT Simons Palmer), St Luke's Agency, Nigel Barrow, Graham Harris and Ian MacArthur (Barnet Williams Partnership), Paul Watson and Simon Mannion (McCann-Erickson), Kevin Morris, Kevin Ferry and Nick Taylor (Grey), Simon Welsh and Tom Geens (Rapier), Jeremy Golding and Yuk Man (WWAV Rapp Collins), John McWilliams, Richard Mummery, Peter Hope and Tim Allan (Arc Advertising), and Chris Hill.

Introduction

Among other things, my father was an exorcist. You might have called him an unofficial or amateur exorcist, because nobody paid him to do it. But he got a steady stream of clients – if that's the right word – none of whom he turned away. My mother gave them tea and biscuits, then my father would cast their demons out. It could take a whole afternoon, and occasionally damaged the furniture.

It was hard to concentrate when this was going on, so I'd often take a football into the back garden, and here one afternoon my father broke the news. He'd just won a skirmish with the Forces of Darkness – an exertion he liked to chill out from with a snooze in the sun – and was shaking his deckchair out when he said casually, 'The Lord spoke to me this afternoon. He told me he's going to end the world before I die.' Then he rolled up his trouser legs and went to sleep.

Now, talk about Doomsday wasn't unknown in our household. The topic came up most weeks, and we meant Doomsday with a capital D – the cavalry riding over the hill, God shouldering his way into history and closing it down like a bar-room brawl. So while the announcement of a date took me by surprise in one way, in another I was primed and ready for it. I seriously expected God to call time. *Before he died*? Well, my father couldn't live *that* long – 20 years, 30 at the most. Like an innings of the England cricket team, it could all be over before tea.

I won't bore you with a long, sorry tale of disappointment. My reckoning came, but only in the form of school exams, after which I was dispatched not to Paradise but to university. And although my father lived a good span, at no time did the clouds part or the fiery chariots descend to collect him. Maybe he hadn't heard God properly? (It's true he was a bit deaf.) Or maybe some crisis blew up in another universe and plans for Doomsday had to be shelved. I don't know. But the fact remains that, like all its predecessors, my father's prophecy tripped on its laces and fell chin-down in a puddle.

All of this, of course, makes a survivor's guide to Doomsday sound about as relevant as lifeboats on a sofa. You might as well read a survivor's guide to blancmange. And yet, and yet ... I've never quite forgotten that biblical Catch-22 my father was so fond of quoting: that the defining feature of the world's end is its *unexpectedness*. Doomsday slips its bank card into our locks just as we're kicking our shoes off and heading for the patio with a beer. Nothing is so sure to make it happen as the absolute certainty that it *won't*.

On this reckoning we're all in the gravest danger. On the other hand, in an age of ever-expanding consumer choice we might ask which precise brand of Doomsday is most likely to hit us, and how – given this uncertainty – we can achieve a reasonable spread of protection. What will the warning signs be? What precautions can we take that won't bend our micro-managed lifestyles out of shape, or incur large drycleaning bills? Such was the agenda awaiting this book.

I have done my best to scratch information together and present it in a useful form. The research has been thorough (at least, it took a long time to do, which counts as the same thing). And where I've had to resort to fibs and mendacious half-truths, I've tried hard to make them interesting. The result should not be construed as an attack either on orthodox Christian faith or on the idea of spirituality, both of which I broadly support. And if you find the advice completely useless when the real Doomsday strikes – well, feel free to write and complain. I'll reply to every letter I receive. And that's a promise.

AN END TO WAR.
AND LEAKY PENS.

THE END OF THE WORLD. IT'S NOT ALL THAT BAD.

DOOMSDAY – THE AD. Paul Young, Art Director; Ben Kay, Copywriter (Abbott Mead Vickers Advertising Agency)

1

Ten to One on 11 August (maybe)

The Prophet of Glory had taped up a little notice outside his flat. In case he was out at the shops, it said, the postman should know that at 12.50 p.m. GMT exactly on 11 August 1999 the world was coming to an end. Women who were with child should be especially careful. Also investors. Next to the notice sat a banner of St George and a sticker for the NSPCC.

I hesitated before ringing. I was here on what anthropologists call *field research* – but that wasn't how it felt. The Prophet had great ambitions. Entrusted with the divine eviction order, he'd written to almost every key player on the planet. The Queen. Tony Blair. The *Los Angeles Times*. Finally tiring of polite refusals – and still determined to get the media on board – he'd placed a million-to-one bet with bookmaker William Hill. So here I was – 'the media' – about to play my part in the Final Mission.

You think you can spot a prophet by the bits of locust stuck in his teeth? Think again. The door opened to reveal a gaunt, middle-aged man in a monogrammed cardigan and slacks. We shook hands, and he followed me into the living room with an aluminium tea trolley so tiny that he had to bend double to wheel it along. An Irish film crew had been here yesterday, he said. Seamus the producer had told him he was 'a natural'. Luckily the programme was due for screening before history came to an end. 'Do you take milk?' he asked. 'By the way, call me Matthew.'

And so the story came out – the story beginning with the *Death of Ron*.

Ron had been Matthew's bosom buddy, a man he'd faithfully looked after through years of psychiatric illness, a stroke and a final, fatal heart attack. Bereavement had hit the Prophet hard. The funeral, he said, had been a fiasco. First the parish priest had refused to take part. Then the funeral firm, though royally appointed ('Not because of me, but because of Princess Diana,' Matthew added modestly), had failed to tell him the time of the service. It had all been, sighed the Prophet, 'a most massive cock-up'.

And then something happened. Something which showed him that Ron's was no ordinary death – that his buddy's 'shuffling off this mortal coil' prefaced nothing less than a Call to Glory.

'On the morning of the funeral,' he said, 'in the early hours, I had the most tremendous shaking. At the time I took it to be pre-funeral nerves, because I had to stand up and read a piece of poetry, which at that time I wasn't very good at. But next morning I found it had left me with a couple of stigmata.'

He flashed his palms at me.

For anyone not up on their saints, stigmata are marks corresponding to the wounds of Christ. You collect them a bit like stamps, though as far as I know you can't swap if you've got two of the same kind. Cases are rare but well documented. Benedict of Reggio got the scratches from the crown of thorns. Hieronyma Carvaglio had the spear wound, which bled every Good Friday. Francisco Forgione got nail marks in both hands, and Francis of Assisi amassed the whole set. Most recently – on Good Friday 1926 – Theresa Neumann received stigmata which spread slowly from her hands and feet to cover her side, shoulders and brow. They never suppurated, but they never healed either.

TEN TO ONE ON 11 AUGUST (MAYBE)

'Show me again,' I said.

Holding his hands out, Matthew pointed to a faint liver spot on the palm, and something I couldn't see in the crook of the other thumb. Possibly stigmata – or just as possibly an accident with a felt-tip pen. Matthew proudly rubbed the marks with his index finger. 'They're very prominent,' he said. 'There's a purple colour, and also a lump has appeared.'

But this was only the beginning.

'After the funeral,' he continued, 'I came back and just sat here in total silence until 9 o'clock. Then I went to bed. But I didn't go to sleep. I know the time because I've got a clock radio. At exactly 3.45 a.m. there was a pulling sensation' – Matthew made a gesture like someone removing a tarantula from his chest – 'on this left-hand side, as though something were being sucked out of me.' He leaned forward slightly, eyes narrowed. 'And I heard myself internally saying, "Ron, *I'm dying!*"'

'You felt,' I said, 'that you were following Ron into the grave?'

The Prophet nodded. 'I now know that the man I *used to be* has departed with Ron. I've been reborn. And we are back together – I in body and he invisibly, as The Holy Spirit.'

'Ron is the Holy Spirit...'

'With a capital T,' he corrected me. '*The* Holy Spirit.'

And here Matthew's face melted into an ingratiating smile. He said with quiet assurance, 'Ron is here at this moment. Outwardly what you see is a typical 55-year-old. But *inwardly* what's happening is very different.'

He described how, when he lay down, Ron's presence manifested itself in surges of pins and needles ('Not pins and needles, but *analogous* to pins and needles'). Also his eyesight had become four-dimensional.

'Anyway,' he said, resuming the story, 'once I'd been reborn I decided to make some changes. That's when I changed my name. Until then I'd been called Malcolm.'

DOOMSDAY

In the circumstances a less modest soul would have gone the whole hog and called himself Jesus. Why change Malcolm to Matthew? The reason was disappointingly mundane: with 'MRD' emblazoned on so many of his sweaters, changing his name to, say, Stanley would have been unduly expensive. 'Plus,' he said, 'it saves a lot of trouble with credit card companies.'

But not, as it turned out, with Barclays Bank, who insisted on taking copies of his old and new signatures (which were identical), and then not only insisted he pay cash for this service, but also, to the Prophet's dismay, overcharged him by a pound. Matthew detected in this small injustice the shadow of global corporate fraud ('If they rip me off for a quid, they may be up to nefarious things on bigger deals'). But he didn't dwell on it. His story was nearing its climax.

'Then,' he said, 'came *the* call from God.'

He paused, seemed to qualify this a little.

'Obviously he didn't say, "*Hello, Matthew, I'm God.*" It was a telephone message on the 1471 number – the one that tells you about your last call.'

Being an optimist, Matthew takes full advantage of British Telecom's 1471 facility. After all, just imagine having the President ring you for details about Doomsday, and *not knowing because you were out buying the groceries*. Had God literally phoned Matthew up?

He leaned forward again, looking searchingly into my eyes, speaking more slowly now. 'I dialled the number and she said, "*You were called today at 12.50 p.m.*" There was a crackling sound, like static. Then she said, "*The caller is waiting for you.*" And then she recited the months of the year, the numbers 1 to 31, and all the days of the week.' The Prophet of Glory held my gaze. 'Now I believe unequivocally that that was *the* call from God.'

In my mind's eye I saw a tape deck seizing up somewhere deep inside a London telephone exchange. How, I asked, had he deduced from this that the world was about to end?

'Well,' said Matthew, 'I checked my blood pressure.'

'Your blood pressure...?'

'I had a blood pressure machine here, obviously – it was Ron's. It was 128 over 76. So whatever this message was all about, it wasn't sending me into a panic.'

'But God didn't – ah – say in so many words that he wanted you to go out and tell people about the world ending.'

Matthew laid a hand on his Bible, one of a number of objects – jigsaw piece, Iris Murdoch novel, chunk of crystal, several Easter cards – laid out on his coffee table like holy objects in a shrine. 'It's like this. One's got to interpret the word. I can't believe that was any kind of hoax. It was my cue to prepare the way.'

'But why *you*?'

'That concerned me for a long time,' he acknowledged. 'I've got a Jekyll and Hyde discussion personality. I haven't got a split personality, but I can argue with myself. I had to work very hard to convince myself that greatness had unexpectedly been thrust upon me. It's awesome to say it, I know. But that's the truth. All the way along I thought I was only looking after a sick man and holding down a job. And I'd end up a lonely old bloke of three-score years and ten, or whatever. Whereas now [again the gently confident smile] I'm expecting an end of a rather *different* kind. On 11 August next year at 12.50 p.m. GMT, these former things will pass away in the twinkling of an eye and this once fine planet will be no more than a black hole in the old universe.'

He didn't pick the date by screwing his eyes shut and sticking a pin in a history book. Way back in the sixteenth century the astrologer Nostradamus gave July 1999 as the terminal month, with an 11-day adjustment that – lo and behold – ties neatly with a solar eclipse. To this Matthew has added the 12.50 p.m. GMT, confirmed by the two additional coincidences of the garbled 1471 call and the fact of his father's watch having stopped at exactly that time. The watch is pinned to the wall like a moth.

We're already winding down to destruction. AIDS, of course, is a clear sign that the world is going to end. So is pollution. It won't take a jiffy to collect a full hand of biblical signs. 'And after that the San Andreas Fault gives, and one nanosecond later everybody on the planet will be either in heaven, or—' Matthew reaches to a high shelf and takes down a box of matches '—in the place represented by *these*.'

Matthew knows which way *he's* going. 'On that day Ron and I will be reunited in the flesh ... in a twinkling of an eye *I will give birth to Ron*.'

At the end of Matthew's universe, then, stands a bereavement reversed. For now safely housed in Matthew's body, Ron will finally be reborn so that friendship can resume in exalted form. I'd intended to ask what Matthew would do if his prophecy failed, but clearly the question had no meaning for him. He was heading for the airport, ticket in hand. There was no Plan B.

'I've got out of all speculative investment,' he told me as I left. 'I'm running down my capital. It's all or nothing. I've organized my finances, and I've booked into a hotel in my birth town on the night before. So I'll finish my existence virtually where I started. I shall turn everything off in this flat, lock the front door, and that's the last time this place will see me.'

Inevitably I found myself wondering how the Prophet of Glory would spend the afternoon of 11 August 1999. After writing hundreds of letters to alert the world's great and good. After applying to receive the Nobel Prize for Physics as discoverer of the long-sought Top Quark, which is, he claims, none other than God himself. After placing a forlorn advertisement in the *Daily Telegraph*. After – finally, and in some desperation – laying the bet on his prediction, as a result of which I and an Irish film crew came to interview him.

TEN TO ONE ON 11 AUGUST (MAYBE)

He shook my hand affably, and I drove back through the weekday traffic into the centre of London. In Matthew's scheme of things, London is the New Jerusalem. 'No other city than this one has a square mile [Revelation 21:16] and pavements proverbially paved with gold [Revelation 21:21]'. Like William Blake, the Prophet has a patriotic streak: the future glory of the City is latent in its very dimensions. 'Pity,' he adds, 'about the litter.'

A couple of days later he wrote to me. In fact he's been writing to me ever since. The envelope bore another cheery reminder to employees of the Post Office: *'Keep at it, Mr Postman. The Universal Struggle is almost over.'* Over the signature, *Matthew Ronald Dumbrell*, the note inside wished me a peaceful heart as I 'helped alert the citizens of this dying planet to the little time left before the Appointed Moment of Judgement and Re-Creation'.

So there: the media's done its duty.

2
Horrible Things about to Happen

As end-time visions go, Matthew Dumbrell's is pretty unfussy: you tick off the signs, then – bang – you're in heaven or hell. But if you believe – as many do – that the blowing down of the universe will be prefaced with a good deal of huffing and puffing, the question arises: *what exactly are we in for?*

In answering this, people like Matthew Dumbrell will usually refer to the Bible, and in particular the book of Revelation. Which immediately lands us head-down in the tar pit. Reading Revelation is a bit like watching TV with the sound turned up and the aerial pulled out. Its language, complained the commentator R. H. Charles, is 'unlike any Greek that was ever penned by mortal man'. And as for content – well, the jury's not so much out as on vacation.

In case you've never tried to read it, the book comes in two parts. The opening consists of seven e-mailish messages aimed at churches floundering in Western Turkey. Then, after a short breather, it's Apocalypse all the way to the end – a string of almost incomprehensible visions, revealing (as the author puts it) 'what must take place after this'. If you're someone who enjoys doing 5,000-piece pictureless jigsaws, you might like to get a Bible down and read the original. For everyone else there's a summary at the end of the book (see Appendix I). Revelation is

Godzilla-meets-Battle-of-the-Somme: stars plummet, cities collapse, hordes of people get slaughtered. For special effects it wins the Oscar every time. As for the script, take a fairly typical section from the end of Chapter 14:

> The angel swung his sickle on the earth, gathered its grapes and threw them into the great winepress of God's wrath. They were trampled in the winepress outside the city, and blood flowed out of the press, rising as high as the horses' bridles for a distance of 1,600 stadia.

What does it mean? Well, on one level: if you plan to buy your wine from God, go for the Chardonnay. Yes, I know, God doesn't *really* have a winepress, and if he did he wouldn't use it to make blood. So perhaps the winepress is figurative – a way of saying that God's wrath will result in copious bloodshed? Well, a few minutes' sweating with a calculator tells us that in a radius of 1,600 stadia (roughly 300 kilometres), and with 200 completely pressed bodies needed to make a single cubic metre of blood, God would need 57,648,620,000,000 people on hand to produce the desired effect, even assuming the ground was watertight. OK, so maybe the numbers are figurative too. Maybe the blood's figurative. Maybe the horses and the grapes are figurative. But *then* what does it mean?

The rise of the prophecy-wonkers

For many centuries the book of Revelation – indeed the entire Bible – was thought to be so problematic that only Approved-and-Trained-Persons could be trusted to read it. Today's Approved-and-Trained-Persons occupy departments of theology, and most of them take a pretty killjoy line.

The FATPROPHET
PROPHECY MIXER ™

HAVE YOUR VERY OWN DATE FOR THE WORLD TO END – PLUS REASONS! NEVER BE STUCK IF SOMEONE ASKS YOU "WHEN IS DOOMSDAY?"! HAVE THE SATISFACTION OF KNOWING THE OTHER GUY'S WRONG!

All you have to do is choose from the options given. Then do the simple calculation beneath to reveal your winning world-ending date! Don't delay, time's ticking away! Fill in your FATPROPHET **Prophecy Mixer** ™ today!

✷

TO CALCULATE THE DAY:

1 Choose a significant date: e.g. founding of Quebec, 1608.
2 Calculate the difference between this and the current year.
3 If the result is positive, subtract 666.
4 If the result is negative, add 666.
5 Divide the new number by seven, ignoring the remainder.
6 If it's a Sunday, add 2, otherwise add 9.
7 Divide by the Prophetic Numerator: 42.

You now have the EXACT NUMBER OF DAYS REMAINING before history ends!

FATPROPHET Prophecy Mixer™ is a trade mark of FATPROPHET End-Time Cards & Gifts. All rights are reserved. Individuals found to have correctly calculated the date without prior purchase of the FATPROPHET Prophecy Mixer™ will be prosecuted. For general inquiries and technical support see listing in Yellow Pages.

*B*ecause thou hast

- sinned greatly
- disregarded the fire safety regulations
- a personal odour problem
- gone on record with a complaint
- - a la vista, Baby

and hast shown no

- remorse
- intelligence whatever
- decent sitcoms for over a year now
- interest in thy food
- yellow cards before half-time

thus saith

- thy financial adviser
- the chairperson of the Ninth Galactic Council
- a recent opinion poll
- Santa
- Reg Chasnett of 28 Spood Avenue

"*Yea*

- verily
- probably
- on balance
- if I feel like it
- just possibly if my ulcer's playing up

unless you

- repent
- deposit $5m in Swiss bank a/c # 98662335
- stop picking your nose
- show a more respectful attitude
- plant cucumbers

I shall

- end the world
- turn the world into an apple strudel
- turn you into an apple strudel
- call my lawyer
- go out with someone else

in just ? days from now!"

DOOMSDAY

In essence, they say, Revelation says nothing concrete about the future. It was written in the shadow of persecution, and aimed to help Christians keep their peckers up as they waited for the lions. Relevance to the twenty-first century? Virtually nil.

Approved-and-Trained-Persons, though, are about as popular nowadays as caviar in a trucker's lunchbox. The modern approach to Revelation is even handed and democratic: if you can breathe, you can hold an opinion. The Bible is fair game for comment, in exactly the same way as the presidency, the monarchy, or the state of Australian cricket. And nowhere has this happened with greater vengeance than in the United States, where the right of the ordinary citizen to pontificate on the Bible (as well as to carry a high-velocity machine gun) is emphatically underlined in the Constitution. In this leisured and largely unprofessional environment, a whole new, streetwise approach to the apocalyptic has arisen. It's called *prophecy-wonking*.

Prophecy-wonking means *taking it upon yourself to figure out the true message of biblical prophecy*. We could add *without having any particular training to do so*, since in prophecy-wonking having people treat you as an expert isn't directly linked to knowing what you're talking about. More often it follows from being on television, running your own web-site, and generally spouting off with more punch and pizzazz than the next guy. Clearly prophecy-wonkers vary in the amount of skill they bring to the task, but five rules seem to be pretty widely adhered to. If prophecy-wonking's the life for you, then don't even think of picking up a Bible before you've grasped the basics:

1. **Decide what the Bible says BEFORE you read it.** Forget soul-searching and scholarship. Do it the easy way. Once you've mastered the technique, you'll be amazed how – over 2,000 years ago – biblical writers had the foresight to back your point of view.

2. **Find verses that support you, and quote them ad nauseam.** Any view, no matter how extreme, can be justified from the Bible. Use a pink marker pen to highlight pet sentences. Don't read the bits above and below, as this may confuse you.
3. **Downplay contradictions.** If opponents use other verses to counter yours, think of a reason why these other verses don't apply. Accuse them of quoting 'out of context'. If that fails, write your own, new version of the Bible with the awkward bits left out.
4. **Go for simplicity.** Theology is politics. Remember: of two competing interpretations, the simpler one's more likely to sell. The junk-food generation wants its religion in a carton with a free soft drink.
5. **Always believe in yourself.** Theology is still politics. Admit a mistake and you lose both your credibility and your power base. In general, being assertive wins more Brownie points than thinking a thing through – so play to your strengths.

Here's a worked example. Say you want to underline the spiritual value of suffering. You need a fresh angle on this, so you look up the word *cheese*. For some reason, cheese in the Bible hasn't attracted much attention, which means that the field's wide open. You soon discover there are three references to cheese, which is a good start because three's a significant number. Father, Son and Holy Spirit, for instance. Or the Three Wise Monkeys, who must be there *somewhere* in the Old Testament. What's more, the cheese reference in Job – 'Did you not ... curdle me like cheese?' (10:10) – clearly refers to life *shaking people up*.

Now you're on a roll. You turn to the second reference – 1 Samuel 17:18 – where the David of David-and-Goliath fame is told to take bread to his brothers in the army. It adds, 'Take along these ten cheeses to the commander of the unit'. Putting aside the more obvious implication (that it was a case of palm-greasing), you home in on the truth you're looking for: *people who've been 'shaken up' are essential to Commander God's spiritual war effort.*

The third reference, in which David and others actually *eat* the cheese, poses more of a challenge. But hey, two out of three's a pretty good strike rate. Quit while you're ahead.

The end-time almanac

Admittedly, prophecy-wonking hasn't much concerned itself with cheese – perhaps because the only gastronomic allusions in Revelation are to eagles gorging themselves on the flesh of the dead. No. Prophecy-wonkers have greater matters in hand. They're watching the tide of history.

For a while they weren't sure if the tide was moving in or out. Around the middle of the nineteenth century – a period when Americans were feeling pretty chuffed with themselves[1] – most prophecy-wonkers saw the world as getting better and better until at last it would be fit for God to take up residence. Rather like cleaning up the rivers to attract the salmon back in. Not surprisingly, the twentieth century has taken its toll on this, and recently most prophecy-wonkers have come around to the view that the world will now go on getting worse and worse until eventually God has to stop the merry-go-round and kick us all off – a position sometimes dubbed *pre-millennialism.*

This tide-going-out theory dovetails neatly with the doctrine of divine judgement. After all, nobody will take seriously the idea of an avenging God bearing down on a society of happy, law-abiding individuals whose only shortcoming is to be mortal. That's unjust – and Doomsday needs justice like omelettes need eggs. If God's going to put things right, then something has to be wrong – *by definition.* In that way prophecy-wonking's a bit dour: history's going downhill, the condition's terminal, and all you can do is figure out how far it's progressed.

This is where Revelation fits in. You decide how critical things are by holding Revelation up next to current affairs and comparing the two. On the face of it, this seems about as useful as measuring your bank balance with a dish of ravioli. Against the odds, though, prophecy-wonkers have put together a pretty consistent vision of the Horrible Things ahead of us. Few are pure literalists. No one I've come across expects to see a lipstick-red woman riding a dragon like Mel Gibson on a Harley Davidson. To make sense of Revelation, you must first crack the Revelation code. Do that, the argument goes, and the text will give you not dragons and beasts but a sequence of concrete historical events of the kind you might see on CNN. All you have to do is stick it together the right way.

So what Horrible Things do we have in store? Let's start with a couple of things most prophecy-wonkers agree on.

1. The tribulation

Nearly all prophecy-wonking assumes that history's decline will terminate in a period of totalitarian rule known as the *tribulation* – a sort of global Third Reich presided over by the Antichrist. The tribulation will make ethnic cleansing look like a trip to the seaside and generally send the planet into meltdown. In a mere three and a half years the Antichrist will become supreme dictator and deposit his blasphemous behind in the temple at Jerusalem – an event referred to (rather obscurely) as the *Abomination of Desolation*.

Actually, Jerusalem no longer has a temple, but this isn't seen as a problem. According to most prophecy-wonkers, extreme Zionists have a prefabricated one lying around in a warehouse and will put it up the moment they get a chance to demolish the mosque which currently occupies the site.

From here the Antichrist will go on to consolidate his power by making all his subjects receive the *Mark of the Beast*. There is some indication that in its early stages the tribulation may be a good thing for pagans. But as the second three and a half years draw to a close, even pagans will feel the pinch, and when the sky begins to fall it turns into a very bad time for everybody.

The worst time of all comes right at the end, when the combined armies of the planet will assemble in the Middle East to be wiped out by God at the *Battle of Armageddon*. Stock prices will plunge (advisable now, by the way, to get out of futures). The battle itself will engage – many claim – a force of 200 million Chinese, and spill so much blood that by the prime-time news you'll literally have to swim in it. Don't be too alarmed, though. By then – what with the plagues, earthquakes, football-sized hailstones and salt water in the taps – you stand a pretty good chance of being dead already.

2. The millennium

It's at this point – not the year 2000 – that the millennium begins. This is a period of direct rule from heaven. No wars. No famines. No queuing at the check-outs. For a thousand years (if you haven't died in the interim) life will be about as good as it gets. If you *have* died, then naturally it'll be pretty quiet. Even funerals will be a novelty, since the millennium sees a widespread return to pre-Flood lifespans. (According to Genesis, remember, Adam lived to 930, so it's bad news for the pensions industry.)

But all this is the lull before the storm, for the millennium winds up in another satanically inspired (and doomed) mass rebellion, after which the dead come back to life and everyone who's ever lived lines up for a ticket to the Hereafter – everyone, that is, except the *true believers*, who've paid already by credit card. If your name's on the list you get in. If it's not, then lucky you, you get to join the Devil's army in that place of everlasting fire and no cappuccinos, where (according to your theology) you will roast for eternity or be instantly cremated.

Armageddon: how not to be there

On other details, the prophecy-wonkers are wonking out of synch. For evidence of this you need only turn to the internet, where cyberspace has grown a little Armageddon of its own as self-appointed prophecy pundits slug it out over one of the most curious – but also most central – events of the end time. They call it the *Rapture*.

The term is derived from the Latin *raptus*, carrying overtones of plunder, rape, abduction and seizure by birds of prey, all of which are more obviously found in another derivative term, the now famous Hollywood dinosaur *velociraptor*. Interestingly, the Rapture is the only main end-time event *not* mentioned in Revelation, the key reference appearing in Paul's second letter to the Thessalonians: 'The dead in Christ will rise first. After that, we who are still alive and are left will be caught up with them in the clouds to meet the Lord in the air...' (4:17). It turns up also in the Gospels: 'That is how it will be at the coming of the Son of Man. Two men will be in the field; one will be taken and the other left. Two women will be grinding with a hand mill; one will be taken and the other left' (Matthew 24:39b–40).

The prophecy-wonkers take such passages at face value. At some point near the end of time, *true* Christian believers will be sucked up into the air in a kind of mass evacuation. A word to the wise, then: if a *true* Christian believer belongs to your car-pool, *don't let him take the wheel*. I'm serious. It was frequently said in my father's circles – though

I've never been able to verify it – that a certain airline owned by American evangelicals made it a policy never to put two born-again pilots on the same plane, since after the Rapture there'd be no one left to land it.

You'd think, of course, that the mass vanishing of Christians would cause the instantaneous conversion of the rest of the planet. But no. Conveniently, according to some commentators, the sudden disappearance will be blamed on aliens – or possibly some unexplained effect of having a Jesus sticker on the back of your car.

Thus far on the Rapture, most prophecy-wonkers take a similar view. What they disagree on – quite vehemently in some cases – is the exact time the airlift begins. *Pre-tribbers* (that's the lingo) will tell you the Rapture comes first – that it's the curtain-raiser on the tribulation, a pulling-out of the diplomatic staff before the fighting starts. If torture spoils your day, then pre-tribberism's the safe choice: click *NO* at the prompt *'DO YOU WANT TO BE A MARTYR?'* and go straight to a comfy seat in the gallery.

Of course, it may bother you to think of friends and colleagues who've missed the evacuation. But don't worry – the prophecy-wonkers have the answer. Just leave behind a surprise parcel containing the *RAPTURE RULER* – 7 x 2.5 inches of durable vinyl plastic 'designed to never be thrown away ... always to be used by the recipient ... and able to go through the Tribulation of 7 horrible years'.[2]

On the other hand, if you're a *post-tribber* you may wish to keep the ruler for yourself, since post-tribberism puts things in a different order – tribulation *then* Rapture, rather like greens before dessert. You may like to keep it even if you're a *mid-tribber*, backing both horses and hoping to be raptured at half-time. Both these groups expect a rough ride, and the post-tribbers particularly are fond of stockpiling supplies to help them get through it. Neither has much time for the pre-tribbers – partly, one suspects, because they regard pre-tribbers as cissies – and the no-man's-land of cyberspace is piled high with Bible verses and convoluted strings of logic purporting to show that one or another view is correct and the others are a bunch of hooey.

To all this may be added a further view – though a minority one – that the tribulation will never happen anyway. Someone called Nicholas, of the Presents of God Ministry and the *Truth Provided Newsletter*, has gone to a great deal of trouble to demonstrate it. 'This file,' he announces, 'contains ALL the Scriptures that PROVE the truth about the Rapture!!! ... More than 75% of all Christians I meet are unaware of the Scriptural facts contained in this document about the Rapture. ALL were truly SHOCKED after reading it!'

One of Nicholas' main objections to the seven-year tribulation is its unfairness: 'This would literally mean SEVEN YEARS OF PARTIES for all the sinners that were left behind on the Earth!' Not keen, apparently, on other people having parties, Nicholas turns to the Gospel of Matthew and its prediction that 'one will be taken and the other left'. He goes on:

ARE YOU LISTENING???? 'THE OTHER LEFT.' ARE YOU CURIOUS ABOUT WHERE THEY ARE LEFT? THE APOSTLES WERE. GO TO THE VERY NEXT VERSE! 'Where, Lord?' they asked. He replied, 'Where there is a dead body, there the vultures will gather.' Let me ask you this ... Have you ever seen vultures gather around people lying on a beach? ... No, I can confidently say, you have not. We all know that a vulture prefers the fairly ripe flesh of a corpse ... Jesus rather bluntly told them that those people that were not going to Heaven THAT SAME DAY would be left behind DEAD.

So, this is the scorched-earth theory of the Rapture. None of these arguments would be pursued so energetically, however, if there weren't a general feeling among prophecy-wonkers that Doomsday is just around the corner. Whatever's going to happen at the end of the world, they assert, it's going to happen soon. And here we find another argument going on: *just how soon is soon?*

> don't panic it's not the end of the world.
>
> REINCARNATION COURSES
> SAMYELING BUDDHIST TEMPLE
> 01791 305 001

DOOMSDAY – THE AD. Creative Team: Rosie Elston & Mary-Sue Lawrence (Mustoe Merriman Herring Levy). Typographer and designer: Tim Lewis (Unreal). Lettering and Illustration: Lieve Cornil.

3

Dates: a Course in Doom-Monger Maths

At the beginning of the nineteenth century a famous prophecy about the end of the world was made by a chicken. Owned by fortune-teller Mary Bateman, the bird had for some time been laying eggs with prophetic messages on them. Thanks to its efforts, Bateman was already a celebrity. But her fame went ballistic the day an egg popped out bearing the date 1809. Here, surely, was incontrovertible proof that the end was in sight.

Well, wrong again. 1809 passed with nothing more disastrous than Napoleon Bonaparte divorcing Empress Marie 'Not Tonight' Josephine, and shortly afterwards Bateman was exposed as a fraud when an intruder caught her stuffing eggs up the chicken's rear end. She later poisoned one of her wealthy clients and was hanged.

So you won't find Mary Bateman in *Who's Who*. Nevertheless, thanks to her knack with poultry, 1809 joins the long list of dates when Doomsday has been expected. Oddly – since much prediction is based on Holy Writ – the Bible itself dismisses prediction as a waste of time. 'Therefore keep watch,' says the Gospel, 'because you do not know the day or the hour' (Matthew 25:13). Not that this fazes the prophecy-wonkers. Prediction's addictive. Take Edgar Whisenaunt, author of the best-selling *88 Reasons Why the Rapture is in 1988*. Humbled by the arrival of the New Year, did he quietly sink back into obscurity? Not on your life. Within weeks he was promoting the sequel: *89 Reasons Why the Rapture is in 1989*. Strangely, not a lot of people bought it.

To prediction junkies, the Bible's assertion that Doomsday will come *when we least expect it* is just a complex double bluff. The end *can* be predicted, they insist, if not to the hour then to the year, and if you've got any sense you'll take precautions. Think of the Los Angeles quake. If you know the fault line's about to pop, then the last thing you do is go out and stand under the expressway.

Assuming for the moment that prediction *is* possible, what – apart from a chicken – do you need to guess that date?

How to make one plus one equal five

The first answer is a basic pass in arithmetic. Meet Marilyn Agee – one of California's acknowledged experts on Bible prophecy. When I stumbled across her internet site, Marilyn was confidently pinning the Rapture on 31 May 1998. Her banner announced:

The countdown: about 2 months
We are running out of time to get right with God

It turned out that this was good news for the consumer. In view of the encroaching end, it went on to say, both of Marilyn Agee's books – *Exit: 2007: The Secret of Secrets Revealed* and *Heaven Found: A Butter and Honey Star* – were on sale for just $5.50 each plus shipping (California residents add 7.75% sales tax).

But why 31 May 1998? Well, as a self-taught Bible scholar, Marilyn felt she'd discovered some vital clues. Namely the following:

- Measured on the timescales of the Bible, 1998 is the six-thousandth anniversary of Adam and Eve being kicked out of the Garden of Eden.
- It is the fiftieth anniversary of the founding of the modern state of Israel. The number 50 is significant: under ancient Israelite law every fiftieth year was proclaimed a Jubilee – a year in which all debts and land leases were cancelled.
- In 1998 over 30 years had passed since Israel took the temple area of Jerusalem in the Six Day War (1967). Again, in ancient Israelite law, 30 was the minimum age at which a priest could assume duties at the temple.
- 31 May falls on the Jewish feast of Pentecost (from the Greek *pentecoste*, or fiftieth), also called the Feast of Weeks.
- Luke 13:6–9, the parable of the barren fig tree, covers four years. Counted inclusively, these can be taken as the years from the Rapture to the start of the tribulation (1998–2001).
- Daniel 8:14 confirms that 'It will take 2,300 evenings and mornings; then the sanctuary will be reconstructed.' These are the 2,300 days from the start of the tribulation (Feast of Pentecost 2001) to the Millennial Day of the Lord (the Feast of Trumpets, 13 September 2007).
- Thus reckoned, the Millennial Day of the Lord falls exactly 40 years – one generation, in Hebrew thought – after Israel's capture of Jerusalem.

For good measure, we might add that 1998 is what you get when you multiply the 'devil's number', 666, by 3. And if you're still not convinced – which, if you're alive to read this, you probably aren't – bear in mind before you scoff that if you *divide* the number 2,000 by 3, you get the devil's number deluxe: 666.6 recurring. Spooked yet? Well you can't say I didn't try.

DATES: A COURSE IN DOOM-MONGER MATHS

Actually, many numbers in the Bible *do* add up. Also, they often have symbolic value. For example, since the number seven in Hebrew thought denotes divine perfection, it's not surprising that God is shown creating the world in seven days. When the universe came off the production line, the writer implies, it was flawless. By contrast, humanity is portrayed as damaged goods – perfection with a one lopped off. Which is why the Beast gets a treble six – imperfection in a triple dose.

All in all, there are enough numerical loose ends lying around in the Bible that prophecy-wonkers can't resist tying them up. And not just the Christian prophecy-wonkers – kabbalists and Satan-worshippers are at it too. It's a wonkers' equivalent of the crossword.

Given a notebook and a rainy afternoon, for instance, it's not too difficult to work out a date for creation. It's been done hundreds of times. The problem – as with all things numerical in the Bible – is what you do with the gaps and ambiguities. And you can bet your life you won't come up with the same date as everybody else. Alongside the 4004 BC agreed by Usher, Spanheim, Calmet and Blair (no, not that Blair), there are 300 alternatives, all based on roughly the same source material, but ranging from Muller's 6984 BC to Rabbi Lipman's 3616 BC.

Working *forwards* in time, then, it's unlikely that the estimates will fit together any more snugly. Efforts just as strenuous as Marilyn Agee's have linked Doomsday to at least a dozen dates since 1900, so far without success. Will the Prophet Matthew Dumbrell be first to unlock the limo? Time will tell. But if he turns out to be wrong, don't worry. The prophetic bus stops here again in 2000, 2001, 2004, 2012, and probably for a good many years after that. There'll be plenty of chances to jump aboard.

DOOMSDAY

Shopping with the Beast

A more cautious – and rather more Hitchcockian – line in prediction relies not on numbers but on *signs*. After all, though he was chary over days and hours, Jesus painted a fairly detailed end-time scenario, adding, 'Even so, when you see all these things, you know that it is near, right at the door...' (Matthew 24:33).

What things? You have to bear in mind, of course, that one man's sign is another man's lifestyle. Jesus talked about 'earthquakes and famines in various places'. But earthquakes and famines have been going on pretty much without interruption since Jesus died. Has the end, then, been 'at the door' for the last 2,000 years? It's a bit like flying from New York to Melbourne and having the captain tell you every three minutes, 'Next time you see a cabin steward you'll know we're about to land.'

The more compelling signs are the one-offs. Particularly hot at the moment are Bible passages that seem to refer to modern communications technology. Revelation informs us, for instance, that the Beast's sidekick

> forced everyone, small and great, rich and poor, free and slave, to receive a mark on his right hand or on his forehead, so that no one could buy or sell unless he had the mark, which is the name of the Beast or the number of his name. This calls for wisdom. If anyone has insight, let him calculate the number of the Beast, for it is man's number. His number is 666. (13:16–18)

Branded human beings? Nothing new about that: it's happened already in the Gulag and the death camps of the Third Reich. But, according to some prophecy-wonkers, much worse is to come. One post-tribber represented on the internet believes that the Mark of the Beast is already with us. He quotes a Christian engineer who, he says, was involved in the development of implantable microchips. Though intended for animals, the chip can just as easily be used on human beings. Where would such a chip be placed? The scientists found that there were only two places on the body where temperature exchange was fast enough to power it: *the forehead and the back of the hand.*

Now this is very creepy. And it's even creepier when you consider all the ways in which a single implantable, unforgeable, unlosable chip might be seen as preferable to a wallet-load of plastic cards. It's creepy, though, for reasons that have no direct connection with the Bible. Extending the technology of social control in the name of consumer convenience may be a bad idea, but it's a bad idea in its own right. The claim that someone 2,000 years ago said it would happen doesn't make it any worse.

For prophecy-wonkers, though, the approaching cashless society is at best a folly waiting to fall into the hands of evil, and at worst a satanically inspired conspiracy. The same view is taken of the smart card being developed by the Canadian-based corporation Mondex. Unlike credit and debit cards, which use magnetic-strip technology and can only work when connected to a central database, the smart card contains a microchip which you can 'load' with money from your account and then spend more or less like cash. Not surprisingly, at the time of writing Mastercard has a controlling 51 per cent share in Mondex, the other owners all being banks, with the exception of the American telecommunications giant AT&T. The commercial advantages are obvious: more convenience, less paperwork, lower wage bills.

But of course all is not as it seems. Consider the Freudian slips being made by those now in charge of smart card development. For a start, Mondex's *Multi-tech Automated Reader Card* yields the acronym MARC (*marc* of the Beast – geddit?). Also the name Mondex, which supposedly stands for 'monetary dexterity', suggests the Latin root

The Galactic Observer

The universe's best selling quality newspaper

Saturday, January 1st, 2050

Black hole 'ate' five billion stars

Milky Way is 5,000 million years old

Young star in Orion 10,000 times brighter than the sun

'Supercluster' of galaxies is 5 million light years across

40,000 new galaxies created yesterday

Universe continues to expand at 15 million miles per day

Spiral galaxies average 1,000 million stars each

Inside — Quarks · Quasars · Sunspots · Black holes · **Late news**

Earth is dead. A tiny planet orbiting one of the billion of stars in the Milky Way Galaxy was wiped out earlier today by a small comet.

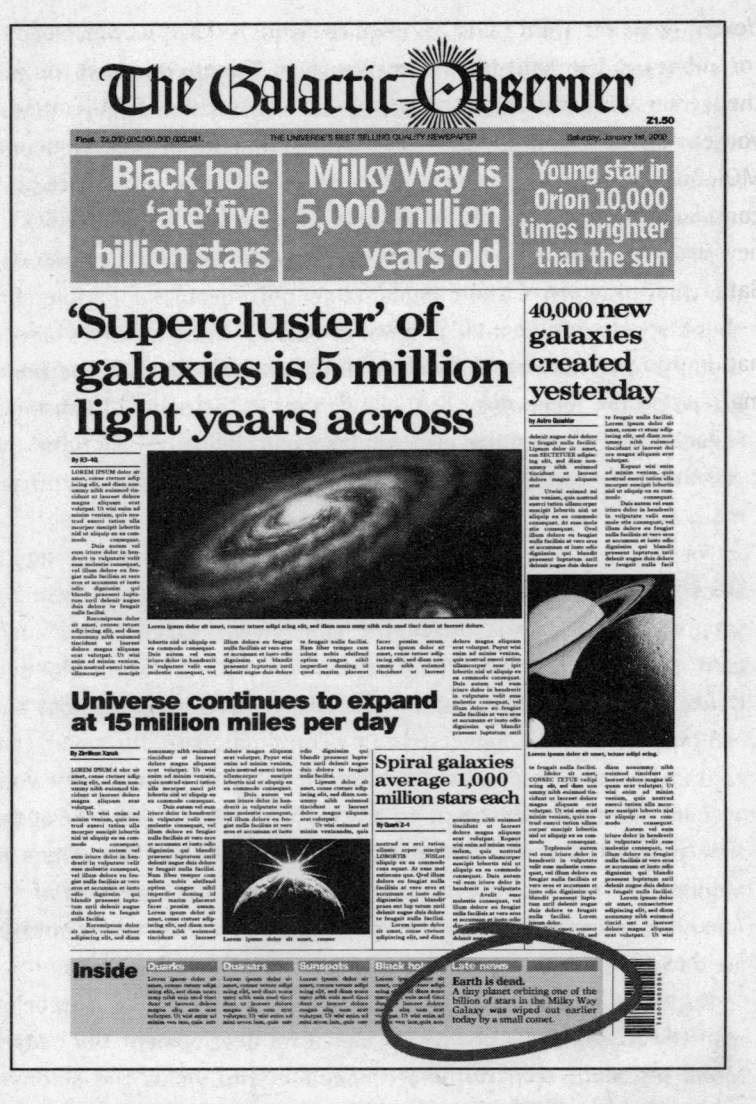

Agency: TBWA GGT Simons Palmer. Copywriter: David Woods. Art Director: Peter Harle. Typographer: Tivy Davies.

dexter, meaning 'right hand', further suggesting that Mondex stands for 'money in the right hand'. The 'Mond' in Mondex surely shadows the French word *monde*, meaning 'world' (as in 'worldly'). Furthermore, you can up the spook factor a couple more notches by unscrambling MONDEX into the anagram DEMON X. And if that isn't enough, consider that the SET in SET MARK, the registered name of Mondex's new internet companion to the smart card, is the Egyptian version of Satan, rendering the real title as SATAN'S MARK.

Such are the arguments some prophecy-wonkers put forward for hacking up your plastic and fleeing to the hills. Of course, if the ultimate aim of all this is global satanic domination, you might ask why the forces of evil are going to such trouble to identify themselves. I guess they just have a wacky sense of humour.

The 666 on your bran flakes

So you refuse the microchip. You spurn the smart card. Never mind – the Antichrist has a third ace up his sleeve: the UPS, or Universal Product Code.

That's the little black-and-white zebra mark tucked away on the underside of your groceries. First introduced in the United States in 1973, the UPC is now standard in Western food retailing. Essentially it's two strings of numbers. The first string identifies the manufacturer, the second the type or make of product. The bars on the code simply represent these numbers in a form that can be read by a laser scanning device and fed into a computer.

So far so good. But look at that UPC a bit more closely. You'll see, say the prophecy-wonkers, that the number strings are separated by three dividers. These dividers are longer than the other bars, but feature a pair of narrow lines identical to those in the code for the number six. Three *unidentified* marks with the value six? The implication's clear: groceries the length and breadth of the Western world *already bear the Mark of the Beast.*

As a responsible citizen, I felt I had to check out this claim. I called John Pearce of the Article Numbers Association, which oversees the administration of bar codes in the UK. Rather confusingly, UPCs in Britain and the Commonwealth are called EANs. Even more confusingly, EAN stands for International Article Number – the 'E' for European being a hangover from the days before Australia and Japan joined up. Briefly I explained the situation with the 666.

'Guard bars,' said Mr Pearce.

'Mm?'

'The long bars at the end and in the middle are called guard bars. They're there to tell the scanner it's a real bar code coming up, as opposed to a checked shirt or something. They say, *Tara! Here's a bar code coming!*'

'Why at both ends?'

'So the code can be read both ways. Otherwise people would be wasting their time at the check-out putting the product round the right way all the time.'

I told him I'd spent some time the previous night getting all the soup cans out of the cupboard and trying to crack the code. Were the guard bars actually sixes?

Mr Pearce sighed the sigh of a man employed to bear fools gladly. 'No. It may appear to the half-dim that the guard bars are sixes, but they're not. What people forget is, it's not just the bars that matter in bar code scanning, but the *spaces* as well. Even the guard bars aren't all the same. The ones at the end are *bar-space-bar*, while the middle one is *space-bar-space-bar-space*. And six is something else completely: *bar-space-bar-space*, along with two other variations.'

'So there's no 666.'

'Getting a 666 out of the bar code,' replied Mr Pearce, 'is so corny it's not worth thinking about.'

Carry on shopping at your local superstore, then, until further notice.

Late, great and still around

To many prophecy-wonkers, no doubt, people like Mr Pearce are satanic spin-doctors positioned to keep the wool firmly pulled over the public eye. On the other hand, I can see why post-tribbers in particular would find such developments alarming. Not for them the divine helicopters snatching true believers to safety as tribulation begins. They know they're in there for the duration.

For that reason post-tribber web-sites lean fondly to mountain-man survivalism. And that's more than just holding your penknife the right way round. Thousands of post-tribbers see wilderness living as their key strategy against the Beast and use the worldwide web to network their cause. People who have their eyes on a cave in the local mountains, then, might profit from a site called *The End Times Christian*.[1]

'If you go into the Great Tribulation,' it asks rhetorically, '(which will start shortly, or some say the 7 years has started) and you and your loved ones are unprepared ... what will you do?'

One thing you can do straight away, apparently, is to buy a copy of *The End-Times Blood Bath* by Robert J. Logston (available online from Armageddon Books), which will 'introduce you to the main players and prepare you for the reign of the Beast'. After that it's straight down to *Captain Dave's Survival Center* for your food and water preservation, weapons procurement, caching, first aid and survival medicine. I found the section on trapping your own food particularly helpful for central London, where you have to nab that waiter before he gives your *fettucini al fungi* to the next table. Also on the site, I noticed, was something called *Dave Lee's Mega Survival List* – which just proves that you never know what you've been up to in a previous life.

Personally – I have to be honest – I find the pre-tribbers more congenial. In contrast to the dour and sandbagged mentality of post-tribberism, the pre-trib camp is in holiday mood. No martyrdom for them, thank you. When Armageddon comes they'll be up in the front circle with their ice-creams and cameras. The big daddy of pre-tribbers, author Hal Lindsey, remembers the moment he found out that the world was going to end. 'I was so excited,' he recalls, 'I couldn't sleep for a week.' Not the comment of a man about to be forcibly implanted with microchips and thrown to the Beast.

As things turned out, he had other causes for excitement, not least the huge sales of his books. Published in the seventies, his *Late Great Planet Earth* sold over 27 million copies. *Newsweek* hailed him as 'the man most responsible for the current renewed interest in prophecy and its relevance to our world today'. Lindsey tackled his prophetic agenda in a broad sweep, taking particular interest in the geopolitics of the Middle East. Twenty years on, though, nothing much seemed to have happened, and to keep the pot boiling Lindsey produced another sizzling bestseller, *Planet Earth 2000 AD*. Had he found, asked one interviewer cautiously, that there was a great deal he had to change?[2]

'Nothing changed,' returned Lindsey robustly. 'But update, yes, a lot. It seems that every intricate part of the scenario that prophets predicted would come together before the return of Christ has advanced significantly. So I found that there was an exciting movement in each one of those categories where things were predicted ... things like famine, plagues, earthquakes, global weather pattern changes, ethnic warring against ethnic groups.'

But while the Middle East remains on a kind of permanent yellow alert, other key elements in the prophetic pattern seem to have drifted out of position. Lindsey's problem – if I can put it like that – is to help current geopolitical realities square up to biblical requirements.

First time round, for instance, he made much of a passage in Ezekiel 38 predicting an invasion of Israel from the Soviet north. Post-Gorbachev, this threat seems to have diminished, and Lindsey sounds like he's whistling to keep his spirits up when he calls it 'exciting' to see the transition of the Soviet Union to a 'regional power ... with a world class arsenal of lethal weapons'. Actually, *exciting* isn't the term that springs first to my mind. How about *seriously scary*?

Also there's the problem of the United States – 'strangely enough, not included in any prophecy that I can find', yet still obstinately prominent on the world stage. From necessity rather than observation, then, Lindsey has to argue that America is in decline. Similar frustrations arise with the European Union, which as a 10-nation revival of the Roman Empire had looked a likely power base for the Antichrist – until expansion east and south messed up the arithmetic. Well, that's showbusiness.

Keep watching that Rapturometer

Of course, there are far more indicators of the end mentioned in the Bible than I have room to shake a stick at here. Anyone interested in keeping track might like to contact a sergeant of the US Air Force called Todd Strandberg. Strandberg's *Rapture Ready*[3] recently won the Best Christian Web-site Award ('If I can do it,' comments Strandberg, 'there's hope for anybody') and tells you everything you need to know in order to predict and prepare for the Rapture.

```
25                    Rapture Red Alert !

20                              Natural
                                disaster

                                  Dodgy new
                                  technology

15                        International
                          incident

                      Middle
10                    Eastern
                      crisis

                        Social unrest &
                        moral decline

 5                  Economic
                    instability

 0                    False religion
    Nov-96  Dec-96  Jan-97  Feb-97  Mar-97  Apr-97
```

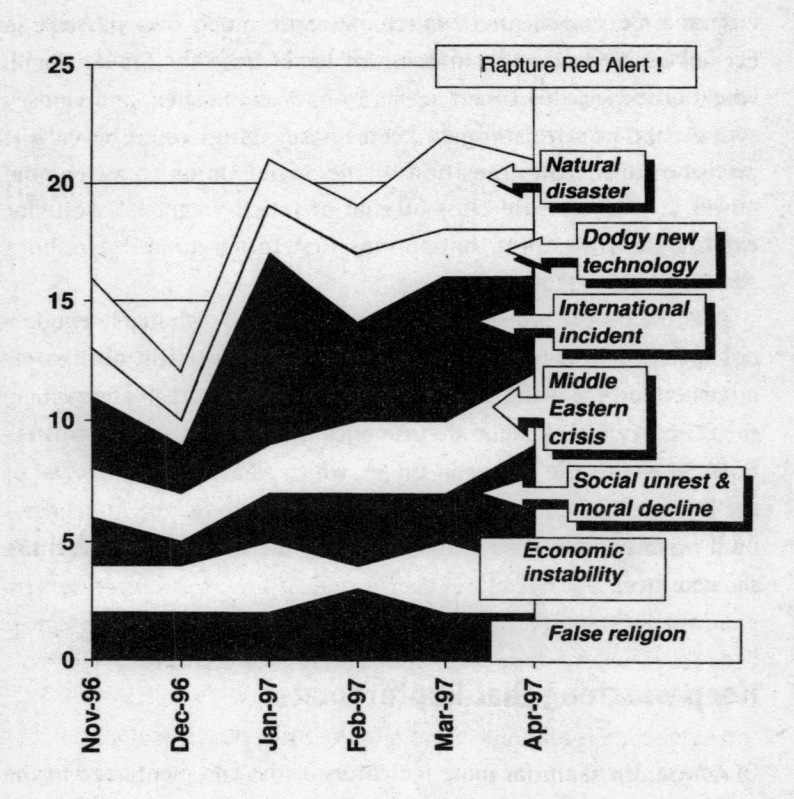

Rapturometer readings, November 1996 to April 1997

One tool he supplies is the Rapture Index – a statistical device to tell you just how likely the Rapture is to happen, given the current background of global events. Updated every month, the Rapture Index uses a scale of 1–5 to rate 'prophetic activity' over 45 different biblical categories. It's so complicated that even Strandberg has given up trying to calculate it. So to simplify matters, let me introduce you to my own (I would humbly say 'improved') version: the *Rapturometer*.

The Rapturometer condenses Strandberg's categories to seven (the perfect number, remember):

NATURAL DISASTER
DODGY NEW TECHNOLOGY
INTERNATIONAL INCIDENT
MIDDLE EASTERN CRISIS
SOCIAL UNREST AND MORAL DECLINE
ECONOMIC INSTABILITY
FALSE RELIGION

Each has a default value of 2, meaning that if we all spent an entire month asleep the overall reading would be 14. Values increase by a point for each Rapture-relevant event occurring in a given category, or decrease if the event is benign. The Rapture Red Alert is triggered if the total score for the month exceeds 25. Actually – I'll be honest here – the number 25 is arbitrary, but it gives you something to aim at.

As you can see from the graph, I road-tested the Rapturometer on the six turbulent months between November 1996 and April 1997 – the lead-up to Britain's last General Election. It took some careful analysis, but I think I got it on the money.

As usual, the combined force of Thanksgiving in the US and Armistice Day had a calming influence on Social Unrest. Unfortunately, however, this effect was offset later in the month by the death of

Britain's popular agony aunt Marjorie Proops. Similarly, in the International Incident category, Boris Yeltsin's open-heart surgery largely cancelled out the re-election of Bill Clinton to the White House – though enough was happening in Zaire to keep the score high. Natural Disaster was pushed up a point by the Channel Tunnel fire.

All the categories plunged in December, making this a quiet month prophetically and notable mostly for its extreme cold (mild Natural Disaster). Come January, however, the combined impact of conflicts in South Korea, Bulgaria, Albania and Algeria (plus Boris Yeltsin's hospitalization for pneumonia) pushed the International Incident category up to a maximum 8. In the Middle East an Israeli soldier sprayed the Hebron market with bullets. Social Unrest should have peaked with the combined deaths of jazz musician Ronnie Scott and China's last official eunuch Sun Yaotang, but later stabilized in the northern hemisphere owing to a rare white Christmas.

Though down on the previous month's total, February 1997 was memorable for events in the minor categories. The Dow Jones Index reached a record 7,000, squeezing the score for Economic Instability. Meanwhile, Dodgy New Technologies featured for the first time with the cloning of Dolly the sheep, and False Religion made itself felt (sorry, personal prejudice here) in the UK's first National Lottery draw. O. J. Simpson was declared guilty by a civil court, but I couldn't make up my mind how to score it.

By the end of March the Dow Jones Index had crashed again, reversing the previous trend on Economic Instability. The Albanian crisis, among other things, reinflated the International Incident category, and Social Unrest took a dangerous upturn with the death of the Rev. W. Awdry, creator of Thomas the Tank Engine – a disaster not even the Oscar success of *The English Patient* could offset.

Social Unrest remained an active category into April, with blockading French fishermen and the death of Donald Shepherd, inventor of the Portakabin (bet you didn't know that). The preservation of the Shroud in the fire at Turin Cathedral put a temporary brake on Moral Decline, masking the shock announcement that, after many years of failure, Screaming Lord Sutch would no longer be standing for election to the British Parliament. Not much happened in the International Incident category, making April a less likely time for the Rapture to happen than March had been, though considerably more Rapture-friendly than the previous December.

As you can see, the whole thing is thoroughly scientific and absolutely reliable. Brits might want to know, of course, what happened to prospects for the Rapture in May, when Tony Blair moved into Downing Street. If so, sorry – I haven't done the sums yet.

What to do if you miss it...

Finally, let's assume the worst. You've boobed. You wake up one morning and your true-believing postman's bag is lying abandoned in the street. A couple of your true-believing neighbours' cars are jammed into your hedge, empty. The TV's gone down because some of the key true-believing technicians haven't turned up for their shifts. Horror of horrors, the prophecy-wonkers were right.

What next?

Todd Strandberg has the answer to that, too – or at least his friend Kurt Seland does[4]. And it's not cheerful news.

The first thing you've got to realize, says Seland, is that tribulation means rising crime. 'Death, brutality and destruction will be part of everyday life. Car-jackings, home invasions, drive-by shootings and bombings will all increase, leaving people with absolutely no sense of security.' It also means bugs. A full set of epidemics – 'AIDS, Ebola virus, flesh-eating bacteria, the return of tuberculosis, incurable gonorrhea, herpes and other sexually transmitted diseases' – ably supported by the typhus, cholera, salmonella and E-coli that'll get you once the water's run out and you can't wash or flush the loo. And don't forget the 'loathsome and malignant ulcer' that's a freebie with the Mark of the Beast.

Still determined to see it through? 'Since you have decided to reject Christ's offer to join the Rapture,' Seland goes on heavily, 'your concern is how to maintain good health in the post-Rapture era. You must build a supply of multiple vitamins with particular emphasis on anti-oxidants such as C and E and minerals. It will also be necessary to have a supply of disinfectants, particularly one that can be added to water to make it potable. Above all, do not accept the mark of the Beast. Did you ever have a canker sore in your mouth? Now think of having canker sores all over your body, on your genitalia, in your mouth. Think how painful and unbearable your life will be. Don't take that mark!'

In the end, your best bet is 'to remove yourself from society and live in a remote area that is difficult to access. Stock up on food, medicines, living supplies, weaponry and gold. You will need enough for 7 years. Don't plan on being able to supplement your food with hunting and fishing because the stocks of wild animals and fish will have been destroyed.' As an afterthought, Seland adds, 'Getting together with a group of like-minded people would provide additional support and safety.'

The post-tribbers, perhaps? Oh no, I forgot – they'll be in heaven already. Bug-eyed and blinking, and with Hal Lindsey and buddies on the next cloud chanting, *'Told ya so...'*

4

Slouching to Bethlehem (the Forensic Case)

Of all the signs of the End, the one that's aroused most interest, fear and speculation is the arrival of Ultimate Evil.

One glance at a newspaper is enough to tell you that evil's pretty old hat. People have been subjugating, raping and butchering one another since the dawn of recorded time, and it's not funny.

To the prophecy-wonkers, though, past atrocities are just a warm-up. Tribulation's on its way and they're manning the periscopes, trying to get an edge on the incoming wave of evil by spotting the man in charge. Because there's no Doomsday without an Antichrist. 'Don't let anyone deceive you,' wrote the Apostle Paul to some nervous believers who thought that perhaps the world had ended while they weren't looking. 'That day will not come until the rebellion occurs and the man of sin is revealed, the man doomed to destruction...' (2 Thessalonians 2:3).

Those are the terms: man of sin, Antichrist. But what exactly should the prophecy-wonkers be looking for? Evil World Dictators don't just pop out of nowhere. Presumably they've been regional dictators and, before that, ambitious colonels, traffic cops and school bullies. I'd even wager that, presented with a line-up of kindergarten kids, you couldn't tell a future Evil World Dictator from a future Easter Bunny ... which leads to a disturbing possibility. You could have met the future Evil

World Dictator already and not have known it. He could be your husband. He could be your dentist. He could be *you*. How on earth could you tell?

The Bible tells us remarkably little about the man himself. Calling someone a 'beast from the sea' isn't exactly swamping us with background, and from that point the narrative in Revelation – if narrative it is – limits itself almost entirely to the actions this individual performs in his seven years at the top. Still, a lead's a lead. And as most people know by now, there's a method of working back from the facts of a crime to produce a detailed profile of the criminal. That method is called *forensic psychiatry*.

I sifted through the Antichrist's story in Revelation and boiled his bio down to the following points:

- Fatally wounded, yet miraculously recovers (13:3).
- Astonishes the masses and acquires a worldwide following (13:3).
- Regarded as peerless and invincible (13:4).
- Given power and political authority by Satan (13:2).
- Like Satan, worshipped as a god (13:4).
- Rules the world for exactly 42 months (13:5).
- Speaks 'proud words and blasphemies' (13:5).
- Engages in acts of religious persecution (13:7).
- Delegates his authority to a media-wise deputy (13:13).
- Relates to the masses through animated, speaking image (13:14).
- Puts to death all those who refuse to worship this image (13:15).
- Imposes the 'Mark of the Beast' on his citizens (13:16–18).
- Defeated at the Battle of Armageddon (19:19–20).

All I needed now was an expert. I made calls to police departments and drew a blank; I made calls to universities and medical schools and drew more blanks. Everybody had heard of forensic psychiatrists – but no one could give me a name. Like Bigfoot, they seemed to have vanished into the ravines, leaving only a trail of rumour behind them.

Pretty soon a High-but-Unnamed-Source in the academic world tried to warn me off. Forensic psychiatrists, he said, were a small but select group, and they were all – ah – rather *difficult* characters. *Difficult?* 'I don't mean they go boozing and betting on the horses,' he added hastily. 'They're just not easy to get along with. And they all *hate* one another. If you want them to do something for you, it's better not to say, "I went to your colleague and he was very helpful." You'd be better saying, "I went to him and the so-and-so was no help at all."'

Believe me, I'm no slacker. But after six months out tracking these creatures I found absolutely zilch. No prints in soft mud. No abandoned fag ends. Not even a fuzzy blob snapped in twilight with a telescopic lens. So perhaps they've all died out, or perhaps the story about them being *difficult* is a kind of masonic smokescreen they put up to give the slip to nosy journalists. I don't know. Fortunately, however, the West Midlands Police finally referred me to an expert of a different kind. Unlike his forensic counterparts, Dr Maurice Greenberg didn't earn his crust wading around bloody murder scenes. And as head of student counselling at University College, London, he seemed well placed to tell me what sort of character the Young Antichrist might be. I presented him with the future Evil World Dictator's curriculum vitae, and invited him to comment.

He took a long look.

'I suspect,' he said finally, 'that what we have here is what we psychiatrists call a *charming psychopath*. To begin with, people will be seduced and persuaded, not bullied. The message will be simple. It will resonate with a feeling everyone knows they've had, but haven't been able to put a name to. People will feel better about themselves when they see this person. They will feel touched. At the same time, of course, he – or she – will incorporate up-to-date technology and use the most refined psychological methods to change the behaviour and attitudes of followers. You will find yourself doing things you'd never have predicted – and *wanting to do them*. Followers will feel benificent as they persecute others, since they know it's being done for a cause. Those who see through it all will be reviled as "out of touch", "yesterday's men", or ironicists. Platitudes, needless to say, will ring out like poetry. "Tough on religion, and tough on the causes of religion." "There will be a new way, a third way." "Trust me; I love you all...."'

Ahem – wasn't there just the faintest Blairite-Clintonian whiff to this charming psychopath? Surely Dr Greenberg wasn't suggesting that just around the corner in 10 Downing Street, just up there in the White House... 'Oh, I wouldn't want you to think that,' replied Dr Greenberg, somewhat equivocally. 'It's just chance...'

So the clues about the future Evil World Dictator may not, in the end, have to do with infant bonding deficiencies or the lack of a paternal role-model. Quite possibly this individual attended a Good School, did sponsored kiss-a-thons, even walked the dog for the old lady next door. Like chickenpox, though, Ultimate Evil gives itself away long before the major symptoms set in. So keep a watchful eye on your friends and neighbours, and be afraid – be *very afraid* – when they say:

'Hey, wouldn't it be fun if our street had its own world government?'

'Hi, you don't know me, but I'm collecting social security numbers for charity...'

'See this scar? Let me tell you about this scar...'

'Excuse me, I'm the devil incarnate. Would you direct me to the United Nations building?'

'Mum, can we have some bar codes and sticky tape, please?'

What will the future Evil World Dictator look like?

Failing psychoanalysis, of course, you might try the simpler method of identifying the fEWD by sight. It should be a cinch. After all, what links the classic villains of stage and screen – Olivier's Richard III, Frankenstein, the Monster from the Black Lagoon? Well, surely the link is that they're all *ugly*. They're *transparently* evil. You know from the moment you see them that they're up to no good.

This *ugly-therefore-evil* principle has been applied to the future Evil World Dictator from the earliest times. For example, the fifth-century *Apocalypse of the Holy Theologian John* gives him the following traits:

- The appearance of his face is gloomy.
- His hair is like the points of arrows.
- His eyebrows are rough.
- His right eye is like the rising morning star.
- His left eye is like a lion's.
- His mouth is a cubit (c. 18 inches) wide.
- His teeth are a span (c. 9 inches) in length.
- His fingers are like sickles.
- His footprints are two cubits long.
- On his forehead is written: THE ANTICHRIST.[1]

Just in case you were in any doubt. A thousand years later, Irish Christianity bought the rights to the fEWD character and the blueprint changed. Thus in the *Book of Lismore*'s 'Story of the Antichrist' *(Sgél Ainte Crisd)* we're told that:

- The length of his body shall be 600 fathoms (c. two-thirds of a mile).
- His body is 40 fathoms in breadth (c. 240 feet).

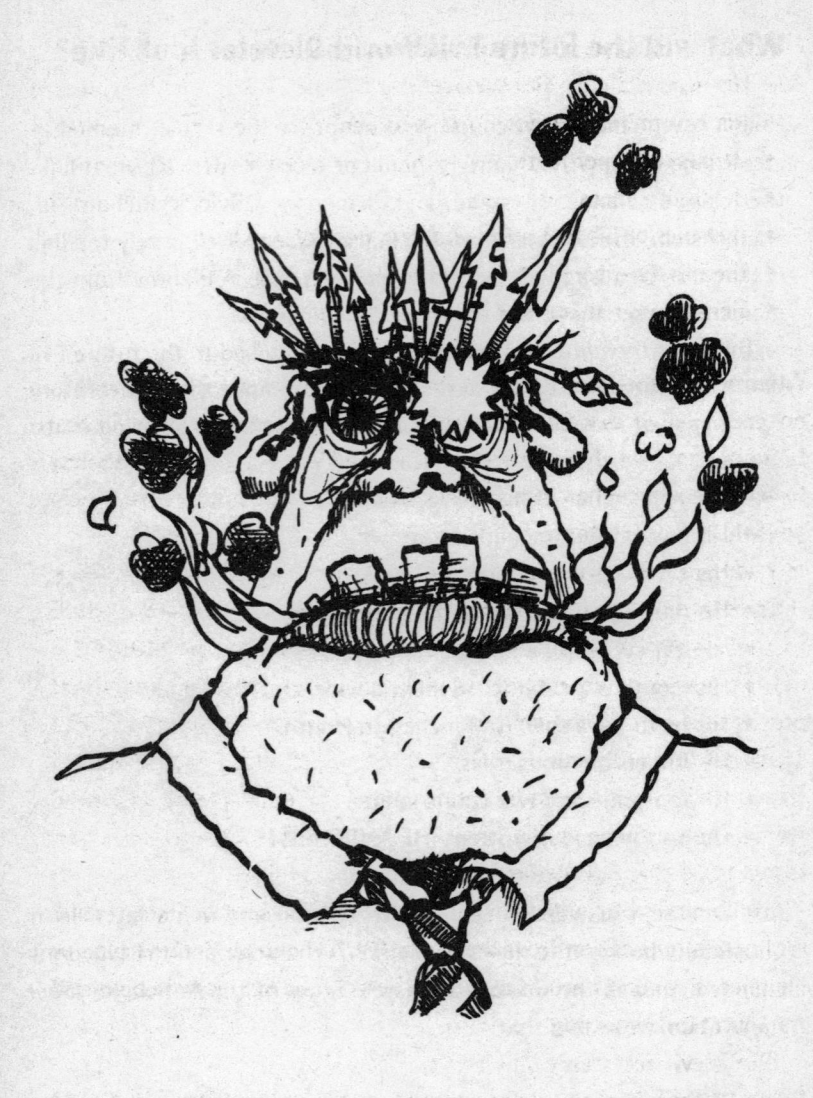

The future Evil World Dictator, based on some medieval descriptions. Does anyone you know look like this?

- He has one eye, which protrudes from his forehead.
- His head is all one flat surface.
- His mouth 'reaches down to his bosom'.
- He has no upper teeth.
- He has no knees.
- The soles of his feet are round like those of a cart.
- There is 'horrible black hair on him'.
- Fiery fumes rise out of his nose and mouth.

Whereas in Disney's animation *Little Tyrant*, being released next year ... no, only kidding. A walk through the gallery of famous Disney villains, though, pretty much confirms the rule – and you don't need an analyst to tell you which character in *101 Dalmatians* eats puppies for lunch. So is there any substance to the link between ugliness and evil?

I took these Antichrist profiles to David Perrett of St Andrews University. As far as I know, David Perrett is the only man in the world to possess both a professorship *and* hair the colour of M&Ms. He defines his research interest as the organization of higher visual processing – in particular how the visual system recognizes facial attributes and understands individual actions. Not long ago he made a foray into the world press by fusing photos of four famously beautiful women into a single image. If anyone knew about ugliness, I thought, it should be him. But ugliness needed careful handling.

'Ugliness and beauty aren't just opposites,' Professor Perrett said. 'Ugliness is a deviation from the norm. The Antichrist's Cyclops eye, for instance, sometimes occurs as a birth defect, and generally people find the mutation disturbing.'

'But is evil necessarily ugly?'

'Well, there's certainly a *perception* of ugliness as evil. Social psychology indicates that attractive faces have *good* attributions – in other words, the person is seen as being more intelligent, more sociable. That's why people with attractive faces tend to get off with lighter prison sentences – because they seem less likely to commit crime. In a similar way, the literature suggests, we tend to make *negative* attributions about people with disfigurements.'

Evidently, then, our attempts to visualize evil rely on a simple psychological fact: that deviations from the norm give us the willies. And the greater the deviation, the more willies we get. At the lower end of the scale are pimply people who don't brush their teeth; at the far end are the Elephant Man and the Antichrist. If we want a fEWD photofit, then, the question might be how many grisly disfigurements we can squash into a single face.

'Suppose,' I suggested to Professor Perrett, 'you merged together, not four beautiful faces, but faces of four indisputably evil people – would that tell us anything?'

He seemed doubtful. For a start there were technical problems. Your indisputably evil people, for instance, have to be snapped frontal, clean shaven, unsmiling, and without earrings or specs. Perhaps it's my lack of faith in human nature, but most indisputably evil people I know don't waste their time posing for photoshoots. And even if they did, there'd be a danger of their various evil characteristics simply cancelling each other out. Besides which, said Professor Perrett, something very similar had already been tried.

'Last century a social scientist went round the prisons and got pictures of convicted criminals, mainly murderers. He merged them all together photographically, and was expecting the result to be systematically different from a second composite that used faces of officers and privates from the army. It was different. But to his surprise the prototypical criminal didn't look ugly at all – he was strikingly handsome.'

According to Professor Perrett, looking evil is no mean feat. 'We've found,' he said, 'that attractiveness is a large concept with several contributing factors – things like age, femininity, expression, apparent personality, even family resemblance. So it's likely that faces look "evil" for a similar variety of reasons. Older faces will tend to look less benign. Eyebrows that are protuberant, creased or furrowed are taken to communicate hostility and anger. Sharp teeth might suggest a predator. And size is important – there's no point in making an evil monster who's only a couple of inches high!

Will the future Evil World Dictator be a beast from the Abyss? Or will he be a thin, callow lad with flat feet and acne? It's a close call. From this point, though, we have no choice but to move onto the $64,000 question: *if* the end times are close, and *if* the future Evil World Dictator is already among us – *then who is he?*

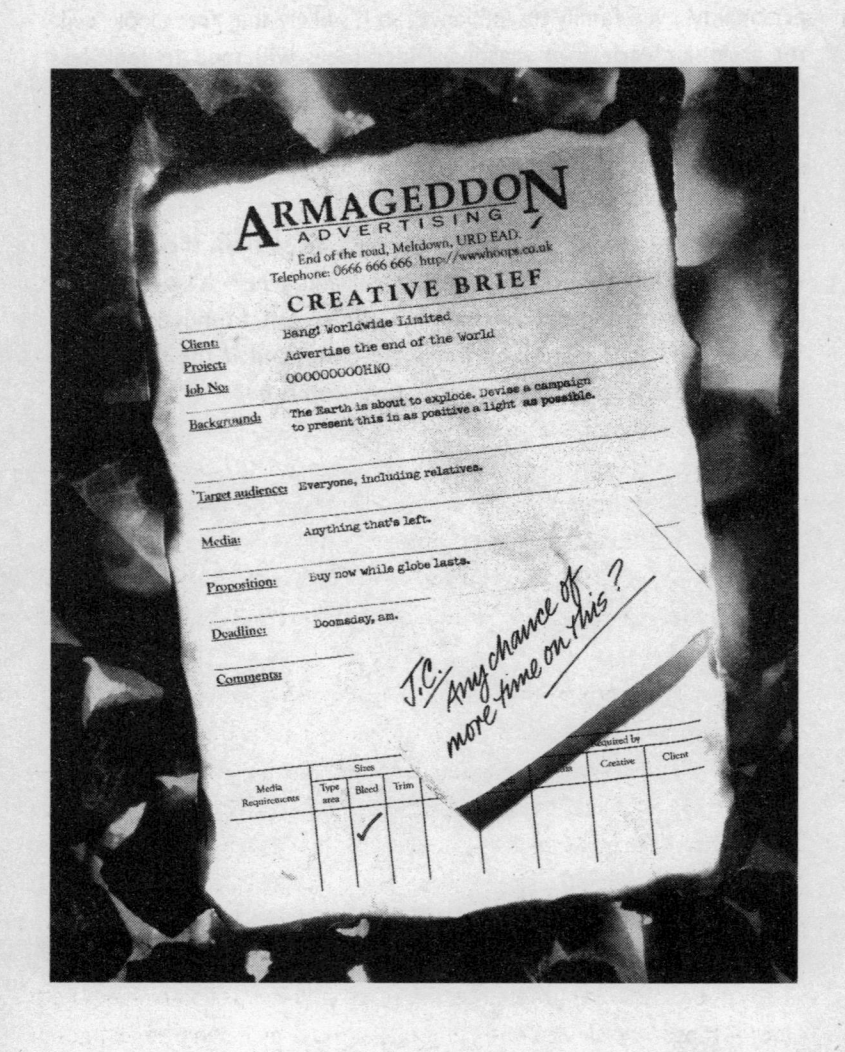

Creative Team: John McWilliams and Chris Hill.   Photography: Richard Mummery   Model Making: Peter Hope   Typography/Retouching: Tim Allan

5

Are You the Future Evil World Dictator?

Baby Face Nelson was a nasty piece of work. Born in 1908, he rose quickly through the ranks of Chicago's organized crime. He did bank robberies. He did vicious killings. He did a stint with Al Capone. Finally he had such a string of impeccably dead referees that the FBI took him on, declaring him America's Public Enemy Number One and kicking him upstairs – with a lot of bullets inside him – on 27 November 1934.

The really disturbing thing about Baby Face Nelson – and also about his contemporary, Charles 'Pretty Boy' Floyd – is that they defy the ugliness rule. If there's an honourable tradition linking beauty with goodness, there's an equally honourable one linking it with vanity, petulance and spite. Nelson could have been a footballer, advertised training shoes, even married a Spice Girl. He was so angelic-looking you could have stuck him on a pack of disposable nappies. He didn't have one eye. Didn't drag a club foot. To use a stock phrase, he *looked good*.

By the same token, of course, we often perceive ordinary Janes and Joes – those *not* blessed with film-star looks – as having honest good sense and hearts of gold. Which leaves us with a dilemma. A plug-ugly, decent bloke might turn out to be the future Evil World Dictator. Or he might turn out to be a plug-ugly, decent bloke. At the same time a sizzling good-looker on a par with – say – Michelle Pfeiffer might be just the sort your mother wants you to bring home. Or she might be the future Evil World Dictator. When the chips are down, science just doesn't give us the tools to distinguish a genuine fEWD from the common man in the street. This is possibly why the prophecy-wonkers can't agree on a candidate.

FEWD – the shortlist

Literally hundreds of names are put forward for the fEWD award every year. Nominations are lodged on a variety of claims. Helpful qualifications are: a BSc in Ruthless Repression, job experience in mass murder, having ambitions to revive the Roman Empire, and having a grudge against the State of Israel. Most people who've gained even an ounce of notoriety in public life will get a nomination somewhere, and the list below, comprising some of most heavily backed candidates, is far from exhaustive. To make it easier, I've given each one a star-rating, from * (rank outsider) to ***** (dead cert). All you have to do is choose.

**** NERO CLAUDIUS DRUSUS GERMANICUS. While Boadicea was leading the British revolt, the Emperor Nero set about rebuilding Rome. This required first burning the city down – a crime he pinned on the Christians, whom he then resolutely punished by having the supposed offenders eaten in public by lions. Desperate for cash to finance his building programme, Nero later denounced his wealthiest citizens as traitors and seized their assets. Among his more charming exploits was kicking his wife to death.

ARE YOU THE FUTURE EVIL WORLD DICTATOR?

* THE POPE. On any day since the Reformation someone somewhere has been voting for the Pope. In some branches of Christianity it's almost an article of faith – even Matthew Dumbrell believes it. Any Pope will do, though some clearly have a stronger track record. The main charges are excessive worldliness and fronting an institution with the word 'Roman' in its title.

** NAPOLEON BONAPARTE. One of a number of leaders (like Charlemagne) with the term *Roman Emperor* in his goals programme. In other respects, though, Napoleon fails to convince. He had no stomach for depravity, never persecuted the Church, and usually retired to bed early with hot cocoa and a biscuit. Plus he got licked at Waterloo.

*** ALEISTER CROWLEY. Promoting himself as 'the wickedest man in the world', Crowley was a Satan-worshipper who surrounded his art with a few extra layers of murky unpleasantness. Not someone you'd hire as a babysitter, but his CV is short of concrete crimes against humanity.

**** ADOLF HITLER. (Automatic entry)

* JOHN F. KENNEDY. As America's first Roman Catholic President, it stood to reason that Kennedy was in the Pope's pocket. He also received exactly 666 votes in the 1956 Democratic convention (yes, it's true). After his assassination in Dallas several prophecy-wonkers expected him to be resurrected. It never happened – perhaps because morticians had removed his brain.

* HENRY KISSINGER. The original shuttle diplomat and broker of the 1973 ceasefire between Israel and Egypt. By a kind of skewed logic, this peacemaking in a region that – according to prophecy – should be melting down into all-out war had to mean Kissinger was an agent of the Devil. Passing up the chance for world dominion, however, Kissinger retired and wrote his memoirs.

**** JOSEPH STALIN. Actually shrewder and more cunning than Hitler, Stalin can point to a record of eager and systematic extermination. Estimates put the numbers who vanished under his rule at around 30 million. Unlike Hitler, he specialized in slaughtering his own citizens.

* KING JUAN CARLOS OF SPAIN. According to the writer Charles Taylor, King Juan Carlos must be the future Evil World Dictator because Spain was the tenth nation to join the EC. If so, democratizing the fascist regime of his predecessor General Franco was a pretty inept start.

** MIKHAIL GORBACHEV. Presiding over the disintegration of the Soviet Union ought to have put Gorbachev out of the running. Nevertheless, he's still widely tipped, mainly because, in the view of some prophecy-wonkers, he already has the Mark of the Beast on his forehead.

*** SADDAM HUSSEIN. A predictable choice. A jobbing tyrant, but eligible mainly on the strength of his power base in the Middle East. If he'd been dictator in, say, New Zealand, he'd have got a good deal less attention. It's notable that no one's put forward names like Pol Pot or Chairman Mao.

** SUN MYUNG MOON. The leader of the Unification Church still claims to be the Messiah. His bid to be future Evil World Dictator therefore rests on blasphemy rather than geopolitical clout. Recently jailed for tax evasion.

** YASSER ARAFAT. Another peace-treaty entrant. When Arafat brought the PLO to the table with Israel in 1993, many prophecy-wonkers thought the seven-year tribulation had begun. As tribulations go, so far it's been pretty quiet. Still, anything can happen.

* LOUIS FARRAKHAN. Leader of the Nation of Islam. No particular reason here – just a lot of people who don't like him.

** WILLIAM JEFFERSON CLINTON. 'A number of folks,' says Todd Strandberg of *Rapture Ready*, 'have e-mailed me saying that Slick Willy is Satan's pet.' The reasons aren't clear. Though Bill Clinton has given new shine to the phrase 'hands-on management', it's hard to see the future Evil World Dictator playing the saxophone. Unless he's the *funky* Evil World Dictator, of course.

***** THE BLOKE WHO CLAMPED MY CAR LAST WEEK. Still in the developmental stage, but shows all the right qualities – vindictiveness, petty officialdom, dead-eyed exactitude, salivation at the sight of pain. Probably you've already received the Mark of the Beast – it's that little crumpled notice telling you how much you have to pay to have the use of your car back.

Of course, a lot of these contenders are shortlisted just for being furthest out on a limb. The most cruel. The most right wing. The most money. Looked at more closely, almost every one of them turns out to have a flaw. Like being dead, for instance. Or not being interested – face it, there's no point in interviewing a man whose only aim in life is to retire and raise pigeons.

Hundreds of feebler candidates, by contrast, are very much alive and just aching for a stab at the limelight. Go online and you'll find fEWDs by the dozen, most of them blending blood-red and dungeon-black in ways that make the text near impossible to read. One to watch is Bob, who's taking Ultimate Evil in a family-friendly direction:

THE LAST POST

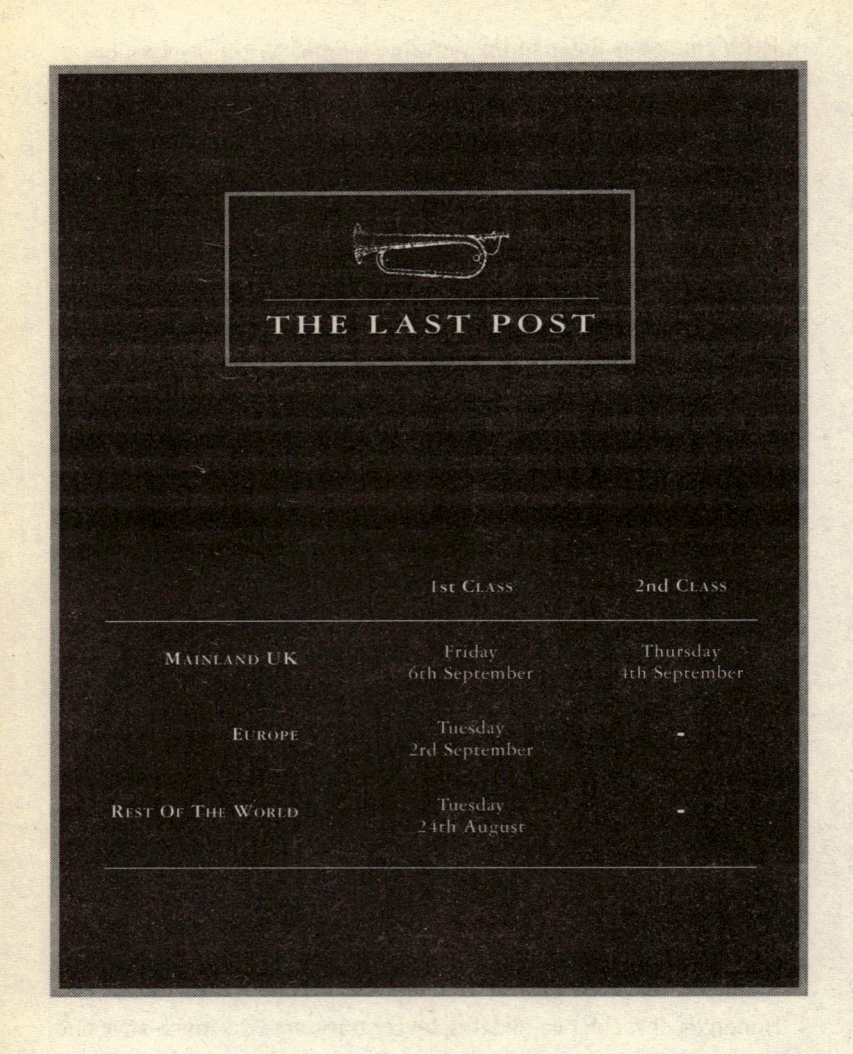

	1st Class	2nd Class
Mainland UK	Friday 6th September	Thursday 4th September
Europe	Tuesday 2nd September	-
Rest Of The World	Tuesday 24th August	-

Agency: St Luke's. 'Client': The Postal Service.

ARE YOU THE FUTURE EVIL WORLD DICTATOR?

> Hi! My name is Bob. I'm the Antichrist. Welcome to my site. I've been trying to get around to creating it for quite awhile, but I have kids and it's hard to find the time. Between taking the children to soccer, scouts, ballet lessons, and school, I barely have enough time to fight Jesus, let alone create a web-site. Yesterday, while I was giving a motivational talk to my minions, it struck me that I was being a hypocrite. I mean how can I motivate the demons of hell, if I can't make the time to create a good family oriented web site? I decided then and there to get it done...[1]

Under 'Fun for the whole family' Bob includes information on 'How to bar-code the baby', complete with rather fetching photo. If families aren't your thing, you may prefer a page attributed to one A. O. Crowley (connection unknown), entitled *Receive thou the Mark of the Beast – official web-site of the Antichrist*.[2] On the whole, for a site dedicated to Ultimate Evil, its tone is rather upbeat. Crowley includes two e-mail pages, which he dubs respectively *e-mail* and *my beloved sh-t-mail*. There's nothing on his *e-mail* page. His *sh-t-mail*, however, is copious and flying at him from all directions. Not far down the page, for example, a correspondent takes Crowley to task for blowing his satanic cover. It concludes:

> In declaring to the world that you are evil and intend to act accordingly, you allow those who serve 'good' to prepare themselves and guard against your assault, whether verbal or physical. Please lean more towards stealth and try to flail a little less wildly in anger.
> Signed: From a concerned Satanist.

A concerned Satanist? But the concerned Christians are after Crowley too. A couple who apparently spend their time browsing satanic sites on the web had this to say:

We read some of your material and realized that Satan has a grip on your soul ... You are fooling around with things that can damn your soul to hell. AO, I pray that you will quit being a silly for Satan and start being a 'GIANT FOR JESUS'.

LOVE IN CHRIST,

                                                    Bob M. & Bruce W.

Well, the list's still open. Maybe somebody known to you is shaping up to be a Silly for Satan? Or maybe you feel you qualify yourself. Either way, cyberspace seems to be the place to post your credentials. On the other hand, before you rush to that computer, you might just want to put yourself through the following simple vetting procedure.

How to enter the prize draw

Actually the task of identifying the future Evil World Dictator isn't quite as hopeless as I've made out. For there is an absolute and objective test on which most prophecy-wonkers agree. It's the *Triple Six Test*.

Pause for a moment while I give you some fascinating-though-useless facts about the number 666, care of the evangelical scholar E. W. Bullinger. A direct descendant of the Bullinger who partnered Martin Luther in the Reformation, 'E. W.' was a maths buff who by a stroke of bad luck ended up as a parish priest. Shocked but not discouraged, he persisted with his hobby and eventually came out with an extraordinary book called *Number in Scripture*.[3] Here is E. W. in full cry on the subject of triple sixes:

> It is remarkable that the Romans did not use all the letters of their alphabet, as did the Hebrews and Greeks. They used only *six*

letters, D, C, L, X, V, and I. And it is still more remarkable, and perhaps significant, that the sum of these amounts to 666:–

1. D = 500
2. C = 100
3. L = 50
4. X = 10
5. V =   5
6. I =   1
   ———
         666

He goes on to outline a number of occurrences of the number 666 in the Old Testament. Then it's back to the maths:

The number 666 has another remarkable property. It is further marked as the *concentration* and essence of 6 by being the *sum* of all the numbers which make up the *square of six*! The square of six is 36 (6^2, or 6 x 6), and the sum of the numbers 1 to 36 = 666, i.e., 1 + 2 + 3 + 4 + 5 + 6 + 7 + 8 + 9 + 10 + 11 + 12 + 13 + 14 + 15 + 16 + 17 + 18 + 19 + 20 + 21 + 22 + 23 + 24 + 25 + 26 + 27 + 28 + 29 + 30 + 31 + 32 + 33 + 34 + 35 + 36 = 666.

They may be arranged in the form of a square with six figures each way, so that the sum of each six figures in any direction shall be another significant *trinity* = 111.

6	32	3	34	35	1
7	11	27	28	8	30
19	14	16	15	23	24
18	20	22	21	17	13
25	29	10	9	26	12
36	5	33	4	2	31

And all that before calculators. What does it mean? Well, probably not very much when compared to the fact that the number 666 provides a clear-cut method of determining if you're Antichrist-positive. Go back to the numbers and letters again. Bullinger is quite right that the Hebrews and the Greeks (who inherited and adapted the Hebrew alphabet) used every letter at their disposal to count with. Not surprisingly, then, every word in these languages can be made to yield a numerical value. All you do is work out the value of each letter in the word, and add those values up. Here, say the prophecy-wonkers, lies the real meaning of that verse in Revelation: 'If any one has insight, let him calculate the number of the beast, for it is man's number. His number is 666' (Revelation 13:18). Clearly, then, if you are the future Evil World Dictator, your name will add up to *the number of the Beast*.

Now this is fine as far as it goes. Hebrew and Greek names all have genuine numerical weights, and any name written in those languages can therefore be tested. Try to do it in *English*, though, and you quickly get bogged down. Unlike their Hebrew and Greek counterparts, English letters do not have numbers linked to them. We count in – well – numbers. So getting the 26 letters of our alphabet to add up needs a bit of sticky tape and glue.

It's not unreasonable, for instance, to give our 'a' the value '1', because 'a' and the Greek *alpha* (α) have a similar sound. The same is true of the second letters of the two alphabets, 'b' and *beta* (β). But which English letter should have the value '3'? The third letter of the Greek alphabet is *gamma* (γ); but the sound of a *gamma* is represented in English by the letter 'g', which comes not third, but seventh. So the prophecy-wonkers had a problem: at a conservative estimate, at least nine of the English letters didn't fit their opposite numbers in Greek, and five didn't fit their opposite numbers in either Greek *or* Hebrew. They corresponded to a different letter, or they didn't correspond at all. What were the prophecy-wonkers to do?

Their solution was elegant: they just ignored it. In most cases, the English letters got the numbers slapped on them that went with their place in the alphabet. And with that, the prophecy-wonkers marched straight to the library and plucked down *Who's Who*. The technique is illustrated below.

To perform a *Triple Six Test*, all you have to do is add up the numbers attached to the letters in your name, and see if the result's a triple six. If it is – bingo – you're eligible for a brand-new hatchback, seven years' global tyranny in the uniform of your choice, two front-row seats at Armageddon and a ticket to the Sauna-With-No-Doors. It's not difficult. Try it. Try it on your friends and relatives. Someone, somewhere out there, is in for a nasty surprise.

Before you ask – no, it's not me. In fact, unless you're very adept at mental arithmetic, it's hard to score a single hit. After two hours with a pencil and pad and a list of possible culprits, I'd only grazed the target:

MAN UNITED FC (668)
HUGH GRANT (671)
ARCHBISHOP GEORGE CAREY (624)

Alarmingly for those Down Under, I discovered that no less than *three* Australian prime ministers (Paul Keating, Robert James Lee Hawke, Gough Whitlam) came within 17 of the magic number. But this competition has no second prizes, and a week later I still needed some creative spelling to find out who might be harbouring the Big Secret:

CHRIS EVAN (666)
THE SPLICE GIRLS (666)

Only after a month of intermittent labour did the crystal ball begin to clear, letting three mysterious and disturbing revelations shine out of the gloom. Make of them what you will. I record them as a matter of scientific curiosity:

    USA TODAY (666)
    R. GULLIT (666)
    PROF. WILLIAM HAGUE (666)

The prophecy-wonkers, though, have been at it a lot longer than I have, and been at it with dedicated software. They noticed early on, for instance, that although Ronnie Reagan failed the full-blown test, his 18-letter name shook down into three chilling groups of six: RONALD WILSON REAGAN. By then, though, the venerable Mr Reagan already had one foot in the history books. So someone else was needed. Someone younger. Someone with unsuspected and sinister potential...

The UK's very own Beast of the Sea

One of the prime prophecy-wonking sites in cyberspace is run by post-tribber Jim Searcy. Given the slaughter in prospect for post-tribbers, Searcy looks forward with surprising relish. His magnum opus has the title: *Great Joy in the Great Tribulation: Simplified Prophecy for the Last Days*.[4] In the hunt for the future Evil World Dictator, many American prophecy-wonkers look first to their own political establishment. Not Searcy: he's got his telescope trained across the Atlantic. His man is the UK's very own Prince Charles.

No, I'm serious. Click on one of Searcy's links, put together by one St Christopher (alias Chris Beard), and you'll find the case laid out in full.[5] 'There are about 40 prophecies concerning the Antichrist,' writes Beard, 'and Prince Charles has already fulfilled over 20 of them. No one else in the world past or present has fulfilled so many requirements.'

Key among these, of course, is pedigree. It turns out that Charles is nothing less than a direct descendant of King David of the House of Judah – 'a hardcore Messianic requirement', explains Beard, and a claim that 'virtually no Jew can make today'. He duly wheels on the detail from something called *The Illustrious Lineage of the Royal House of Britain* (London, The Covenant Publishing Co. Ltd, 1902). Like the Gospel of Matthew, the genealogy starts from Judah, fourth son of Jacob, and follows the biblical line of begatting down through David and Solomon to Zedekiah, the Israelite monarch taken prisoner in 586 BC when Jerusalem was overrun by the Babylonians.

At this point, though, it takes an odd turn. Zedekiah, we are told, begat Tea Tephi, 'ancestor of Irish and Scottish Kings', who in turn begat Ugaine the Great, who further begat Argus the Prolific. How Tea Tephi got among the Celts is not explained. Still, a couple of dozen generations downstream we find his genes swimming around in Robert the Bruce. From there it's all relatively plain sailing through the Stuarts and the Hanoverians until King George VI begets Elizabeth II and Elizabeth II begets (take a deep breath) Charles, Prince of Wales.

Having established this connection, Beard draws our attention to the verse in Revelation that says 'the dragon gave the Beast his power and his throne and great authority' (Revelation 13:2b). Given that this same dragon is earlier described as 'red' (12:3), what else could it be than the famous dragon of the Welsh flag – the very same figure that appeared on the standards of Titus's Roman army which sacked Jerusalem in AD 70? Furthermore, doesn't Daniel speak of this Dictator as a 'contemptible person who has not been given the honor of royalty' (Daniel 11:21)? Charles' coat of arms, he adds, 'is riddled with occultic symbolism' and capped with a motto that translates *I am your man*. No surprise, then, that 'on March 6th, 1996, on CNN, Charles showed the world that he and his sons had been the first people to be voluntarily implanted with a microchip in their right hands for security purposes.'

With this impressive body of evidence assembled, Beard duly puts the nail in the coffin by applying the *Triple Six Test*. And lo and behold, the Prince passes with flying colours:

CHARLES	227
PRINCE	237
OF	66
WALES	136
=	666

No! Could it be? Alas, Beard assures us, the Prince

> is probably one of the most powerful and influential individuals in the world. He and 24 knights make up the Order of the Garter, which is head over Freemasonry. This is how he was able to manipulate 33rd degree Masons Shimon Peres, King Hussein, Bill Clinton, George Bush, and Maurice Strong, to mention a few. He is behind three of the most important documents of this decade, the UN's Global Security Programme, the 7-Year Oslo Accord, and the Rio Summit's Agenda 21. The holdings of the House of Windsor include Archer-Daniels-Midland, which controls 75% of the world's grain. He can decide what nations eat or starve. The Prince's World Business Forum of 200 top corporate leaders consolidates 26% of the world's wealth. You would find it hard to believe the list of owned corporations.

Of course, Beard allows, 'some people don't think Charles is this capable or even intelligent'; rather the Prince is perceived as 'a harmless, gentle, and kind man'. But in the world of Christian conspiracy theory you can take nothing at face value. Time to call in Mulder and Scully.

...and the Beast from *Jurassic Park*

As a postcript, one more blast from the information superhighway. If you're one of that sad band of individuals with nothing better to do than hang around the windy streets of cyberspace spying on other people's parties, you may have noticed a strange thing. I refer to a gathering swell of unrest against Barney the Dinosaur. In Canada, particularly, the all-singing all-dancing purple reptile from children's TV has aroused such vociferous opposition that a number of hostile websites have been set up, chief of which is probably that of the PDDC (Purple Dino Death Campaign), entitled – rather catchily, I thought – *Death to Barney*.[6]

Promising that you will be 'awakened to the truth', the site offers a set of alluring links, including: *Day of The Barney, Interesting ideas on how to punish the Purple Menace, Jihad to Destroy Barney on the Worldwide Web*, and *The Purple Pestilence Page: actual reasons why Barney is unhealthy for children*. At first this seems inexplicable. After all, there are no equivalent sites called things like *Strangle Dr Suess* or *Fix your Fatwa on Kermit the Frog*. But of course the truth soon dawns. It's official: Barney is the Antichrist.

At least so says a 'a Mensan from Phoenixville, PA'.[7] Laid out in slabs of 100 per cent pure logic, the argument has a cold and terrible beauty about it:

Given: BARNEY IS A CUTE PURPLE DINOSAUR
Prove: BARNEY IS THE ANTICHRIST
1) The Romans had no letter 'U' in their alphabet.
2) The Romans used the letter 'V' for 'U'.
3) Using the Roman alphabet: CUTE PURPLE DINOSAUR becomes CVTE PVRPLE DINOSAVR.

4)	Extracting the Roman numerals from CVTE PVRPLE DINOSAVR, we get C, V, V, L, D, I, V.
5)	Substitute the decimal equivalents for the Roman numerals: C=100, V=5, L=50, D=500, I=1.
6)	Add all decimal equivalents: C=100, V=5, V=5, L=50, D=500, I=1, V=5
7)	The total of the above numbers is 666.
8)	In the Bible, 666 is the Mark of the Beast.
9)	The Beast is the Antichrist.
10)	Therefore...

I read this twice.

Then slowly I clicked back to the PDDC page. Near the bottom was a link button called something like *The Kill Barney Fun Page*. I surfed over to a site displaying an image of the dinosaur and a choice of deadly weapons: knife, gun, axe, uzi, shotgun, motorcycle, cannon. I selected the cannon (best to be sure), and numbly reached out my mouse hand. I closed my fingers around the controls. And then ... and then ... *I did it.* I drilled Barney full of whatever it is cannonballs are made of. It took me seven goes, but I got him good. I know I did, because afterwards a little message appeared over the body saying: *Barney is dead.*

Am I ashamed? No, sir. Prophecy-wonking may be out of my range – but don't say I haven't done my bit to save the planet.[8]

DON'T BE A SHEEP, BE A GOAT

GO TO HELL

Agency: Barnet Williams Partnership. Creative Directors: Nigel Barrow, Graham Harris. Agency contact: Ian MacArthur. 'Client': Hell.

6

What to Wear at the Last Judgement

Shortly after my graduation I took it into my head to visit Canada and applied to the Worshipful Society of Whatsits (the details escape me) in case they wanted to pay my fare. Well, pigs might fly. Anyway, I was determined to give it a shot, and after an all but interminable wait in reception was shown into a large, oak-panelled office, at the end of which sat a single dining chair and a desk with six pinstriped suits behind it. My memory of the next 20 minutes is hazy on all but two things. One, the extraordinary depth of silence that followed my attempt to crack a joke. And two, walking past the next interviewee on my way out and knowing – with almost religious certainty – that the money was going to him and not to me.

I bear no grudge. Not a big one, anyway, because I can see now that the greatest and most fatal of my many strategic errors was to stroll into the presence of six pinstriped suits wearing beige linen, trainers and a Panama hat. That money was gone long before I delivered my numbing joke. It was gone the moment I opened my wardrobe.

For better or worse, whenever I think about the Last Judgement I think also about that ill-fated application. I'm convinced there's a lesson in it somewhere. There's all that stuff in the management literature on the *first four minutes*, for instance. Plus it's been *de rigueur* for some time that swastika-clad defendants turn up at their trials in a jacket and tie. In short: first impressions count. On the other hand, most visions of the end – and the biblical ones particularly – foresee pretty summary justice. No objections are tolerated, no appeals allowed. Of all the self-help scenarios relating to Doomsday, the idea that you might in some way give a good account of yourself as you meet your Maker seems by far the least promising.

Grow as much hair as you can

It was rather in two minds, then, that I went to see Angela Slack. Angela trades under the title of *image consultant*, and is the kind of professional routinely sought out by politicians, media people, business leaders and (had I but known) humble applicants to the Worshipful Whatsits. If she could train up a government spokesperson for grilling on TV, I reasoned, it was just possible that she'd have some useful tips. Angela was reassuringly confident.

'Image is dealing with people's prejudices,' she told me. 'Controlling other people's opinion of you, so that effectively you're in charge of what happens to you. If you've been a bad boy and you want God to think you're good, *you can do it*.'

We were sitting in her apartment in London's SW3. It was roomy and tastefully furnished; you reached it by reporting to a uniformed security man in a gazebo, then crossing one of a number of footbridges across the ornamental pond. Angela had something of the Persian cat about her. She'd kicked her shoes off and curled up with exquisite poise on one of her lush settees. I asked what kind of image I should present.

'Basically I'd advise you to be clean cut – have a nice haircut, nice smile, clean clothes.'

'Like the Mormons?'

'But not so severe. Clean's important, because cleanliness has all sorts of implications. It's like any interview. You have to look as if you care for yourself, that you have pride.'

I asked her about colours.

'Colour is very individual,' she said. 'I'd have to do an analysis of your skin, hair and eyes – predominantly the skin because you see more skin than anything else. Also strength of features. You can only wear high contrasts if you have strong features. Otherwise you get lost.'

Personally, I've always seen myself as a greeny, khaki, burgundy sort of person. I risked this information with Angela, who pursed her lips and assessed me, by lamplight, at a distance of roughly six feet.

'I think that would be about right. Are your eyes blue or brown?'

'Blue.'

'Well, you might be able to go more reddy-bluey than you think you can. Or navy, of course. Anybody could wear navy. Do you tan easily? People who tan easily quite often have a yellower tone of skin. That means you may suit warmer colours.'

So, warm reddy-blueys for me. I asked about style, indicating that I thought God's preferences in this line might lean to the conservative.

'If you were American,' said Angela, 'I'd say preppy rather than surfey. I wouldn't turn up in wildly checked shorts. On the other hand, a Savile Row suit is too square and tucked in – it might give the impression you're hiding something. I'd recommend Italian – softer, rounder shoulder. Georgio Armani would be my choice. You can have a nice T-shirt, an Armani suit and loafers with no socks. You want him to think you're gentle.'

In half an hour we covered a great deal of ground. Make up ('Keep your eyes open and see what the angels are wearing'), cologne ('Go easy on it'), facial hair ('Keep it under control') and what to eat before you go ('You don't want to get there with a piece of carrot stuck in your teeth'). All the advice seemed sensible. But something told me not to rush into a decision, and I plumped for a second opinion.

Unlike Angela, my next consultant was low on the cuddly quotient. Mary Spillane comes from Massachussetts, and in another life would probably have been a New York lawyer. Her office shows evidence of work-in-progress. Ceiling to floor on the wall behind her desk are book jackets, press clippings and celebrity photos. She talks fast. And, to my surprise, she seemed to have an inside track on the Coming Interview.

'It's going to be snap judgement,' she told me. 'God has the balance sheet on all of us, and he's a quick worker. But I think he wants to be *sold to*. He's facing an eternity with billions of righteous goody-two-shoes, and I think that reality has soaked him up big-time into providing some leeway for the marginal characters. Not the real nasties. Artful Dodgers. Lovable rogues, people who, if they'd had a mentor or a guiding light, would be running the Bank of England. It's the luck of the draw they weren't, but they're still good to their mothers.'

I pondered this Dickensian picture of Paradise. Meanwhile, Mary Spillane had raced on.

'So,' she said, 'we should think about presenting ourselves as an *asset for eternity*. We're going to be on God's team. He wants to be able to call on us to fire the troops, to get things going so it's not going to be a drag for him.'

'In terms of clothing, then...' I said, trying to come back to the question.

'Formality has no role here. We're going to forget anything businesslike. I would suggest you go in looser-style clothing and in pastel colours. Right shade, of course – you don't want to look sickly or ill. But loose clothing, a creative style, nothing too loud or brash. Natural fibres. Leathers would be fine. White leathers. A white leather suit.'

If I'm honest, white leather boutiques aren't the ones I head for first on payday. Mary wasn't going all the way with the Elvis look, though. I'd thought maybe a pair of sunglasses would go nicely – but no.

'They're not advisable. The Lord has X-ray vision, and anyway shades are just so sinister.' No beards, either. A senior man prefers a clean-shaven face. 'And let's face it, God's just like any other chairman of the board.'

She sounded very certain about this. But then Mary Spillane sounds certain about everything. We moved on to attitude.

'Element of deference,' she said. 'Element of *Delighted to meetcha. Been lookin' forward to meetin' ya. You're the big dude in the sky I've been dyin' to see.* You see, enthusiasm's going to go a long way. There'll be so many who just go and kiss his feet and all the rest of it. You want to stand out. So: enthusiasm, good eye contact, positive body language without being aggressive. Also listen. Be inquisitive of him. Because probably no one ever asks him any questions. *So how's it been going for ya? Have ya had a good time? Any jobs ya need done?* Play him a little. See how well he opens up and give him what he needs. If he wants to bare his own soul and tell you what a lousy time he's had for the last few thousand years, then sit down, suggest you have a beer, discuss it. Maybe he'd like to take a break, put everyone else on hold, refer the next candidates to Peter and the boys.'

This kind of cosy one-on-one felt like something a woman might do better than a man. Were there qualities a woman might usefully bring to Judgement Day?

'Well, we know that God is asexual,' said Mary crisply. 'So there's no point in trying to play the sex card. But you could fulfil a couple of different roles. Maybe the Queen Mother. All smiles – you know, you'd want to just cuddle up and smell that lavender, a real big cosy mama. Or you may want to play the kid sister, the cheerleader, positive, on your team, full of can-do and energy. Maybe a little overwhelming at times, but they'll need that type – there's so much dead weight up there. Overall I'd say: be feminine, be different, be sensuous, and grow as much hair as you can. Do that, and I think you'll have an anchor with God.'

'And what if *God*'s a woman?' I asked.

'I couldn't care less,' replied Mary Spillane. 'I'm a lapsed Catholic.'

But some people *do* care. Readers of august religious journals like the *Church Times* will tell you that there's a heated debate going on as to whether God has a tender, touchy-feely feminine side as well as a thunderbolt-toting, macho, masculine one. It's sexual theology. You may choke on the prayer *Our Mother Who Art in Heaven*, but the charge that generations of male clergy have turned God into a projection of their own misogynistic selves at least deserves a straight answer. Does the gender issue have any bearing on survival at the Last Judgement? I thought I'd give the interviewing one last stab. And where else to go for a decisive view on womanhood and Doomsday than the Bible of transgender-relationship-management, *Cosmopolitan*?

The foot-stroking solution

Like most males, I've had my closest encounters with *Cosmopolitan* in the doctor's surgery. You thumb your way through a five-year-old copy of *Farm Equipment Weekly*, gaze at posters about meningitis, and finally pick up *Cosmo* because it's the only fresh item on the pile and anyway you've always wondered what women say to one another between the covers of their glossy magazines. Half a dozen pairs of eyes track you as you pick it up. You ignore them, trying your best to look spontaneous and casual. And then – wouldn't you know it? – the darn thing falls open at a feature on breast enlargement.

With such limited research behind me, I had no idea what to expect of *Cosmo*'s editor, Mandi Norwood. I'd vaguely pictured round spectacles, water-retention problems and a double chin. This proved inaccurate. In almost every way Mandi Norwood embodied the ethos of her publication – a vivacious and attractive woman who managed without the slightest suggestion of effort to give the impression that she found interviews *fun*.

I began by airing the views of my two image consultants. Did Mandi Norwood feel good about the Armani suit and loafers?

She laughed. 'Personally I think anything would be an improvement on the long white sheets and halos that they all wear. I think it depends on what makes you comfortable. I'm always at my wittiest and sparkliest when I'm wearing high heels. I'm not suggesting that for you. It just depends what makes you feel great.'

I confessed to doubts about the white leather.

'Oh, I don't know – there's something about it that's sexy without being really tarty. White leather's soft. Quite kitteny. Quite humble.'

'You think I should go into the Last Judgement looking *kitteny*?'

'Kitteny but not brazen,' she affirmed. 'Of course, it depends on whether it's a white leather G-string. But a soft white leather coat – that kind of thing would really suit you, actually.'

At this she gave a completely watertight smile. For Mandi, I discovered, smiling would be a major resource on Judgement Day should God turn out – as expected – to be male. 'If you smile you can literally get away with anything. It's that sparkle in your eye and that mischievous grin that overrides everything. Whatever you're wearing, however you walk. The power is in the smile.'

'Other women seem cautious about "playing the sex card".'

'Oh yeah, that's a definite no-no,' said Mandi. 'But there's a difference between playing the sex card and that lovely flirtatious way that we have with each other. And women flirt with women – so if God turns out to be a woman you can easily flirt with her too. I think it's lovely to flirt in an interview. I think God would be up for a little bit of flirtation.'

In the event of God being a woman, though, what – apart from flirting – would the average man have to do to prove himself worthy of heaven?

'Stroke his partner's feet regularly,' replied Mandi, so promptly that I had to ask her to repeat it. 'There isn't a woman alive who doesn't like foot stroking. And be courteous, kind, sensitive and respectful at all times. You see,' she explained, 'men have a false impression of what women want from them. What women really want is a man who is clean, for a start. Who actually brushes his hair and his teeth. They don't like men who have halitosis and psoriasis, and yet still have this unbelievable conviction that they're God's gift to women. That's just the worst type. What women look for is someone who's honest and modest, self-deprecating without eating too much humble pie, someone chivalrous but not too snakey. But clean is a good start. Clean is a very good start.'

'And if you were God, who *wouldn't* you let in – apart from pushy men with psoriasis?'

'Probably those hideous estate agents who take single women around flats and are incredibly patronizing. All men who patronize you over property, mechanics, technology and science. And men who finish every sentence with *sweetheart*.'

I suggested adding internet nerds to the list. Surprisingly, though, she wouldn't have it. 'No, they're fine. Each to their own. Internet nerds are okay.'

I'll just repeat that, in case you missed it. The editor of *Cosmo* says *internet nerds are okay.*

'It's the internet sex pests that we don't like,' she added.

'And what about men who take footballs to bed with them – I mean, who leave you at the shops every Saturday afternoon?'

'Oh, we don't mind sporty men. And as for Saturday afternoons, you just bugger that and go shopping anyway. In fact, it's better shopping without a man unless he's absolutely rolling in it.'

Clearly, if she gets a job at the pearly gates, Mandi Norwood's going to give men a hard time. And it won't stop when they get inside.

DOOMSDAY

Vomiting your vindaloo over the golden pavements is – understandably – out. So, oddly enough, is washing up. 'But I'd certainly have them on hand for rubbing in the old body lotion and suntan cream. Men are very, very good at that. They're also very good at leaping across hot sands to get you a drink.'

On balance this seemed a rather slim skills base. You get to heaven with your MBA and mobile phone, and the only job on offer is beach-waiter-cum-masseur. 'Aren't men good for anything else?' I asked.

Mandi Norwood thought for a moment. 'Yes,' she said. 'They're good at blowing up lilos.'

Hot hints for your holiday in heaven

As I say, I'm not hopeful that there'll be much leeway when the real Judgement's on. Doomsday may come like a drugs raid, at five in the morning. The department store may be closed just when you need that new pair of loafers. But on the off-chance that your image is worth working on, *and* that you have time to work on it, here's what you have to remember:

- Take a bath.
- Get a haircut (or not, if you're a woman).
- Don't be caught in polyester, viscose or latex.
- Bin those shades.
- Take a short counselling course.
- Buy some Queen Mother videos. Study them carefully.
- Get those high heels you always wanted.
- Smile, smile, smile.
- Find a foot and practise stroking it.
- If you're an internet nerd, stay cool.

WHAT TO WEAR AT THE LAST JUDGEMENT

- Eschew estate agency as a career move.
- Flirt freely, but address only one woman per day as *sweetheart*.
- Blow up every lilo you find.

7
Aliens are a-Comin'

Go out in the dark and look up. What do you see? Well, clouds, yes. But on a clear night? What exactly is that frozen screensaver stretched overhead?

Confident that all significant action happened right here on earth, scholars in the Middle Ages would have seen only empty, concentric shells of space. Not any longer. The earth we once thought of as a kind of Times Square has turned out instead to be a remote piece of hillbilly country on the fringes of the galactic metropolis. No buses come this far; *Time Out* on Alpha Centuri omits to mention us. But make no mistake: sooner or later someone's going to come motoring across space with a bottle of fizzy drink and a sandwich box. *And then the jig's up.*

Some think the jig's up already – that the aliens have already been. Frankly, I'm not convinced. Yes, I know about Roswell, and several of my friends assure me they're abducted by aliens every other weekend. But real evidence? Apparently it's all mopped up before the press can get a camera to it. UFOs, which you might expect to see zipping past the Hubble space telescope, seem instead to be visible only to woolly-hatted men standing on hilltops in New Mexico. Strip away the speculation and conspiracy, in fact, and you end up not with *proof* but with *probability* – the idea that in a universe this big there must, surely, be more than one planet with creatures able to scratch their armpits and think. Beyond that, science will not commit itself.

Nevertheless, the thought of alien picnickers setting off in our direction has caused a good deal of excitement. Even such seasoned observers as Graham Birdsall, editor of *UFO Magazine* and by his own confession a 'feet-on-the-ground kind of guy', seems hard put to distinguish genuine sightings from hallucination and hoax. I asked if he thought there really were alien ships out there. His reply was, 'I'm pretty convinced that there's a wealth of evidence that supports the view that some, and I stress some, of a small residue of inexplicable reports could be of an extraterrestrial nature.' *Pretty* convinced? *Some* of a *small* residue? *Could* be? This is the voice of a man with his back against a wall.

Take, for example, the choicely named comet Hale-Bopp, visible in our skies at roughly the time when Bill Clinton was beginning his second stint at the White House. Briefly, the hullabaloo surrounding the comet's visit unfolded like this:

1. In November 1996, as Hale-Bopp sails towards a (relatively) close encounter with the earth, backyard astronomer Chuck Shramek from Houston, Texas, detects a second luminous object which appears to be flying alongside. He takes a picture of it.
2. Impressed with the image, Shramek quickly broadcasts his discovery. He puts the image on his web-site and appears on Art Bell's radio programme *Dreamland*. This 'companion' object, he says, has a slight flare of light running through it. He describes it as 'Saturn-like'.
3. The discovery sets cyberspace buzzing. Hundreds of Usenet messages are posted, and a couple of dozen new web-sites appear containing online parodies and inspirational poetry and art. On his home page, Whitley Strieber wonders if this companion object might be an 'incoming starship full of aliens'. The Farsight Institute,

LEARN TO PLAY THE HARP IN JUST 5 DAYS!!

The REDEMPTION Co

☎ **0999 123 4658**

'Preparing you to meet your maker'.

Agency: McCann-Erickson (London). Copywriter: Paul Watson. Art Director: Simon Mannion. 'Client': The Redemption Co.

a firm that specializes in 'remote viewing', commissions a clutch of psychics to project their thoughts onto it. One of them sees 'an artificial, metal structure, not on earth', adding that 'the Galactic Council, or some higher order, is watching very interested...' Other commentators identify Hale-Bopp's companion as the twelfth planet (no mention of planets 10 and 11) or as a harbinger of the Apocalypse.

4. All this comes to the attention of the scientific community, including Tom Bopp and Alan Hale, co-discoverers of the comet. A battery of 'debunking' web-sites appear, on one of which Hale endorses the prevailing professional view that the comet's companion is nothing more than a bright ninth-magnitude star, the 'Saturn-like' appearance being caused by a 'diffraction effect' familiar to anyone who knows about *real* astronomy.

5. Undaunted, Shramek replies with the accusation that Hale, NASA and the Vatican are all involved in a massive Hale-Bopp cover-up. 'Months before I took this picture,' he asserts, 'I knew there was a strong effort underway to keep good pictures of the comet away from the public.'

6. By now Hale-Bopp's companion object has been dubbed *Hale-Mary*. Mysteriously, in view of Shramek's claim of a cover-up, web photos of the comet apparently posted *before* the discovery of Hale-Mary suddenly start to show a bright blob in roughly the same position as the companion in Shramek's photo. Whitley Strieber and Art Bell receive an impressively clear exposure showing Hale-Mary 'nestled deep in the comet's corona'. It comes from a 'mysterious astrophysicist' who 'prefers to remain anonymous'. Whitley Strieber confidently calls Hale-Bopp 'a fabulous turn of history for us, the luck to be found in this vast dark universe, never to be alone anymore'.

7. By mid-January 1997, however, these images have come into question. University of Hawaii astronomer Olivier R. Hainaut shows that Hale-Mary was *added* to Strieber's and Bell's picture, 'most likely using digital image processing techniques'. Hainaut should know – he snapped the original, undoctored image himself.
8. None of this fazes Hale-Mary's discoverer, Chuck Shramek. On his web-site he wonders aloud why the Vatican should be operating an observatory at the University of Arizona. Answer: the 'Pope-Scope' is aimed at Hale-Bopp.
9. Shramek's suspicions are deepened by an anonymous letter faxed to Art Bell. Signing himself 'a priest', the writer claims to have stumbled on a top-secret Vatican project dubbed 'Wormwood', involving a 'direct link-up to the Hubble space telescope'. The Holy Father, he says, is 'very aware of the existence of the companion, and is *very* worried about it'. Soon after liberating some encrypted messages from the Vatican's computer database, the priest found Vatican contract assassins on his tail. Soon afterwards, his parents were 'killed in a car crash in France' and his brother and sister 'killed when their single engine plane went down on the east coast of the US'.
10. Late January 1997. Asked about the Hale–NASA–Vatican conspiracy, a spokesman at the Arizona University's observatory claims never to have heard of Shramek's accusation. As the comet closes, Hale-Mary sceptics comment, 'We have no plans to clean the bathroom and vacuum the apartment.'
11. In Spring 1997 comet Hale-Bopp passes without incident.[1]

Are aliens nice?

Of course, there is a good deal of fun to be had on the internet by playing the part of a renegade padre and telling someone like Chuck

Shramek that the Vatican's out to assassinate you. But the joke only works because it's believed – because there are people out there so hungry for alien contact that details like common sense and verification can be put in the fridge for later. They know the arrival of that first interstellar picnicker will be the end of the world as we know it – and they desperately want it to happen.

But will the picnickers want us crawling all over their sandwiches? Clearly those tracking Hale-Bopp and Hale-Mary don't expect to be swatted with a rolled-up newspaper. In all probability, they think, the aliens are not here by chance at all, but have crossed the universe with the specific aim either of observing us or of helping us hatch. Like zoologists filming mountain gorillas, they keep their distance. Nonetheless, the human–alien relationship tends to be described in intimate and fluffy language: brotherhood, friendship, healing, advancement. Aliens are our buddies. They are tolerant, restrained, able to take the long view. If they find us sniffing their eclairs they will gently break off a corner and let us stuff ourselves.

One of the more famous flying saucer groups in America is Unarius. It started in 1954 when Ruth, later the leader of the movement, met her husband-to-be at a psychic convention. Clearly a master of the chat-up line, Ernest told Ruth that in a previous life she'd been the Pharaoh's daughter who rescued Moses from the bulrushes. From there the romance blossomed, Ernest receiving clairvoyant transmissions from the seven spiritual planets, and Ruth typing them up for publication. In 1965, having so far enjoyed only a modest following, Ruth and Ernest 'began to get more fully in touch with their past lives as Jesus and Mary Magdalene', and when Ernest died in 1971, Ruth, who was soon crowned Queen Uriel, Queen of the Archangels by the form of her dead husband, penned a further 13 visionary books under the title *Tesla Speaks*. In their review of the group, academics Diana Tumminia and R. George Kirkpatrick record:

In volume two, ascended philosophers and scientists, like Plato, Socrates, and Isaac Newton, lent their voices to praise Unarius. The third volume holds the channeled wisdom of John F. Kennedy and Dwight D. Eisenhower, among other statesmen ... Volume seven of the *Tesla Speaks* series is entitled *Countdown!!! To Spacefleet Landing*. Aside from messages from George Adamski and Orfeo Angelucci on the planet Venus, and good wishes from the dead astronauts Grissom, White and Chaffee, a 'revelation' dated March 17, 1974, states that Uriel was informed that a 'spacefleet landing shall be instituted mainly for the purposes to inform the earth people of his great Intergalactic Confederation Project now being formulated...'[2]

It's amazing how much less pernickety people get when they're dead. But then by 1993 Uriel was dead too, so presumably she was able to put her case direct. Anyway, the date set for the landing is now 2001, Uriel's hundredth birthday, when she will return not only to enlighten humanity but to retrieve her mothballed and beloved Space Cadillac. The touchdown will usher in a new golden age of 'logic and reason', beginning when 'vehicles of light' descend to bring higher knowledge and gifts of technology to earth. The starships, it is said, will land on top of each other. At the resulting saucer tower, the Space Brothers will set up a hospital and university. In total they will bring 33,000 interplanetary scientists who will work for the betterment of all humankind, a task they will commence by recovering the lost libraries of Atlantis and Lemuria.

It's easy to sneer, and California is, well, California. At the same time, this idea that the space fleets are not only 'out there' but 'out there and rooting for us' seems to beg a lot of questions. The reasoning goes: MORE TECHNICALLY ADVANCED → MORE MATURE → MORE BENIGN. But this isn't the way it's worked in our own history. Based on experience, a more realistic projection would be: MORE TECHNICALLY ADVANCED → MORE POWERFUL → MORE PRONE TO POLICIES OF BRUTAL SUBJUGATION. What makes us think the aliens' intentions are honourable?

The stock reply is that alien civilization has advanced to a point where they recognize antisocial behaviour as backward and counter-evolutionary. No selfish genes for the aliens: time and past mistakes have propelled them to enlightenment. Aliens never drop their rubbish in the street. Alien boxing has been declared a non-contact sport. At home, female aliens never complain of headaches, and male aliens stroke the females' feet for hours without once dropping off and snoring. Aliens, in fact, are saints.

Well, maybe they are. More likely, though, relentless change has pushed us into a state of hysteria and, as Jung suggested, we cling to the myth of benevolent aliens as a way of dealing with our collective stress. There's a striking resemblance, after all, between Uriel's prophecies and the belief of some Polynesian islanders that time will end with the arrival of a tramp steamer full of cargo.[3] For what are the stacked-up 'vehicles of light' but cargo ships, stuffed as they are with interplanetary scientists and cosmic enlightenment? It's the ancestor spirits coming back to rescue us. In many saucer cults, in fact, aliens aren't aliens at all, but creators, foster parents, mentors. According to Erich von Daniken:

> In the unknown past ... there was a battle in the depths of the galaxy between two space peoples like us. The losers escaped in a spaceship to earth, and built tunnel systems underground to avoid detection by the pursuers. Eventually they emerged from the tunnels and began to create human life 'in their own image from already existing monkeys'. After that they had decided that the evolutionary process was too slow, and in impatience wiped

out 'those who did not follow the biological laws laid down.' Subsequently men began to dig underground hideouts themselves for fear of 'divine judgement'. Eventually the astronauts took off for fresh fields and pastures new, but still they're watching us, curious about the results of their experiment.[4]

So, aliens with time on their hands; aliens literally playing God. And, heck, just knowing it puts a new spring in your step. No more awkward mysteries, for a start. Concerned that our dunderheaded ancients couldn't have pulled off the pyramids? No problem: maroon an alien on earth and he'll turn out pyramids like bored baboons crack nuts. And if von Daniken isn't your cup of tea, there's plenty else on offer – like Stanley Kubrick's *2001: A Space Odyssey*, where the part of the spooky humanoid alien is played by a spooky humming brick.

Oddly, one possibility largely ignored by saucer-theorists is that the aliens never left. And yet this is perfectly plausible. They stopped here to refuel, bred human beings to do their laundry, and had such a great time that they buried their spaceships and stayed. To this day we obediently open doors for them and troop out to the supermarket to buy them food. You think you *own your cat*? Get real.

What to do if you're attacked by aliens

There is no survival issue here, of course. You don't need to survive benevolent aliens any more than you need to survive a warm bath. But what if Uriel and those like her are wrong in picturing feeble humanity getting a friendly, helping hand? What if the reality is that we're doing very nicely, thank you very much – and any moment now the cosmic Vikings are going to beam down, torch our huts and pillage us?

Fortunately, out there in cyberspace S. C. Summers, Mark Godswell and J. R. Mooneyham are already giving the matter some thought. They outline the problem thus:

> We (humanity as a whole) currently suffer from a window of vulnerability. We're sufficiently advanced to attract attention with radio signals as far as sixty or seventy light years away, but woefully inadequate to the task of defending ourselves from anyone who might show up in response. By some five to seven centuries from now we should pretty much be able to take care of ourselves in this regard...[5]

Let's hope so. Meanwhile, with our window of vulnerability jammed open, what are we to do? Heaven alone knows what those creepy aliens are up to. Reconnoitring the planet? Seeing the lie of the land before they invade? They might have secret plans to turn the earth into a bottle bank, to plant Martian cocaine, harvest us for our kidney stones, shear us twice a year for pillow stuffing, suck our blood, or just beat us across the plains for the shooting parties. It's all too horrible to contemplate.

But never fear. Summers, Godswell and Mooneyham are busily gathering the best ideas around, and have posted them on the internet in an article called *How we should repel/survive an alien invasion*. What follows here is a bare summary. Writing in the online magazine *FLUX*, they begin their briefing with what they call 'Special Strategies':

1. **Practise, practise, practise.** We seek special government funding for computer gaming based on scientifically plausible scenarios of alien invasion or domination. 'A great side benefit of this design would be its educational value – if the games were forced to be strictly plausible to qualify for subsidies, those playing with them

couldn't help but learn something of subjects like physics and mathematics.' Plus any incoming alien could be zapped by a three-year-old with a joystick.
2. **Hide.** At least hide our eggs, so we can recreate the human race after aliens have wiped us out. This could be done in two ways. Either pack some of us off to 'a very, very distant system, largely secret from humanity as a whole to protect the effort from discovery by aliens scouring our databases and interrogating our people here'. Or 'install an undetectable artificial intelligence with suitable support technologies deep within the Earth itself, programmed and equipped to do nothing more than hide and survive long enough to outlast the alien occupation'. And gee, if the plan works, we can kill each other and roast the planet with greenhouse gases all over again.
3. **Create a think-tank.** In the novel *Footfall* by Larry Niven and Jerry Pournelle, an alien invasion is thwarted by the government and military bringing together the world's best science-fiction authors, scientists and engineers. 'We would do well to remember this vision,' comment Summers, Godswell and Mooneyham, 'as it could save our collective behinds.' We might, they add, 'also bring in the world's master magicians and illusionists, to help create diversions or misinformation campaigns'.

And don't forget the spin-doctors. If all that fails, however, Summers, Godswell and Mooneyham have a second line of defence: what they call 'Last Resort Possibilities':

1. **Hit them with a satellite.** 'Keep in mind it may be possible to command some of our larger orbiting satellites (or even manned vessels) to drop from orbit on trajectories guaranteed to impact critical alien bases, using significant masses at hypersonic velocities.' Cheaper significant masses, of course, can be dropped with the help of pigeons.

BEAT THE RUSH

E.X.I.T.

Agency: Grey. Writer: Kevin Morris. Art Director: Kevin Ferry. Typography: Nick Taylor. 'Client': E. X. I. T.

2. **Explode a volcano.** Once we've run out of satellites, it might be possible to set off a volcanic eruption or an earthquake. 'Of course, for this to work the aliens must have made their camp in an area conducive to such events. But just imagine the effect on a nearby alien encampment in the 1980s of waking Mount St Helens a bit early with ten to thirty megatons of explosive force.' Failing that, 'could a few strategically placed nuclear blasts divert an already existing hurricane towards an alien camp?' Or – am I being obtuse? – we could just drop the bombs straight on the camp.
3. **Nuke ourselves.** Why didn't I think of that? 'We could mask a major counterattack with an apparent nuclear war amongst ourselves. Sure, we'd pay a high price in destruction to some of our own cities and bases, but it might be the only way to rid ourselves of the alien threat.'
4. **Pretend we're religious.** We delete from our databases all sceptical references to religion and the supernatural, thereby fooling the aliens into thinking there's 'a long term presence on Earth of some other advanced civilization, hidden from easy detection'. The downside is that, once the aliens have fled, the falsified databases would 'vastly strengthen the hand of organized religion and mystic groups across-the-board for years to come, forcing repeated confrontations in everything from economics to politics'. Also, the aliens might be converted *en masse* and stay. Whoops.
5. **Get help from the future.** 'This is admittedly a long shot in more ways than one.' The idea is to send 'software agents' deep into the future to find a way to defeat the aliens in the present. Not being able to travel through time is a wee bit of a problem, but not insurmountable. We just set up a very, very big computer, and when the computer (in, say, 500 years' time) figures out both how to defeat the aliens and how to *tell* us how to defeat the aliens, it sends a message back. Of course, we could bury a bottle with a

note in, explaining our problem, and hope a second Einstein digs it up in the year 9003.

And if the last resorts also fail, here are the 'Special Tactics':

1. **Use public key encryption.** This will stop the aliens finding out what we're saying to one another on e-mail. Also, we should add confusing personal touches to our communications, thus making it more obscure. Something like, 'Did the earth move for you last night?' should put the wind up them.
2. **Look stupid.** 'We could use the pretense of major political upheavals generated by religious and/or environmental extremists to make it appear world governments have set back humanity's technology base by a century or more.' The aliens underestimate us and get sloppy. We gain a crucial advantage. Is 'pretense' quite the right word, though?
3. **Give hackers a job.** This is the 'Trojan horse' method. Our peskiest hackers break into alien computer systems and muck about. Alternatively we make the aliens a gift of what we claim is our very best software – but load it with bugs and viruses. It will help, of course, if the aliens are already running Windows98.

This great work is still unfinished. If you have any bright ideas (or have recently read a sci-fi novel), then Summers, Godswell and Mooneyham are keen to hear about them – 'debugged and easy to apply as possible'. In the event of the alien invasion actually occurring, they add, 'it just could be your idea that saves the day. If this turned out to be the case, you'd go down in history as the savior of humanity.' No free magnum of champagne, though.

8

Doomsday – the Ad (How to Sell the End of the World)

In the media, predictions of the end are invariably treated as a joke. No one buys the idea that Doomsday is just around the corner. In commercial terms, of course, you might say that Doomsday's just a poor product – on a par with (for example) chocolate-covered lettuce leaves or a dippable sponge for drinking beer. But I don't think that's the whole story. You can have a difficult product and still find a market for it – like the inventor of the first square fly-swatter whose sales plummeted until he coined the line 'swat them in the corners'. No. In my view, what's done in Doomsday is *lousy advertising*.

For many years the doom-monger's favoured medium was the sandwich board. He stood on the pavement like a Bronze Age tank. His front said 'THE END IS NIGH'. And the back followed up with 'PREPARE TO MEET THY DOOM'. Now it's true that these phrases have since become miniature classics of cliché. But do they really persuade? When it comes to arousing the feel-good factor they have about the same affective power as a truncheon. They're all hook and no worm.

Admittedly, recent prophets have branched out a bit. Some hand out leaflets. Others set up a web-site. But the message has never shaken off its hole-in-a-corner feel, never really carried. And since Doomsday is a rather more urgent matter than – for instance – the launch of a new breakfast cereal, we have to ask whether Doom-mongery shouldn't go the whole hog and bring in the professionals. After all, the world only ends once. Assuming, then, that God is a reasonably sharp operator, what sort of campaign would he commission to get his point across?

God goes to Saatchi & Saatchi

Deep in the heart of Saatchi & Saatchi is a man called Fish. In case you're not *au fait* with the internal structure of an advertising agency, it consists of two kinds of people. There are the account-handlers, who represent the agency to clients and – presumably being graduates of Mary Spillane – look as if they've just stepped off the cover of *Vogue* or *GQ*. And then there are people like Fish. These are known in the trade as *creatives*. Creatives can turn up to work in grubby sweatshirts and torn jeans because their job is not to front the organization but to produce what finally goes on the hoardings and the TV. Some, like Fish, do things with words. Others do things with pictures. One of each together is called a *team*.

Fish's office had that never-tidied, student feel. I'd called him to outline what I wanted. We were now following standard procedure by setting up a three-way meeting with account-handler Jill Simpson. A conference room was found; coffee was poured; we got down to work.

Fish cleared his throat. 'Now – you're God,' he said.

'Yes.'

'And the world's ending some time next year.'

'We felt it was time to blow the whistle.'

Jill and Fish looked at one another – a sort of I'll-jump-if-you-do kind of look. 'Well,' said Jill, 'I suppose the two key questions at this point are how much money you want to spend, and what you're hoping to make people *do*.'

I hesitated. Naturally, cash wasn't a problem. But as for what God might hope to *achieve* through an advertising campaign – that depended on your theology. I waffled for a bit in a revisionist-fundamentalist direction until we had the outline of an aim. It sat on the table between us like a lump of wet clay.

'It looks to me,' said Jill, 'like we need to do the campaign in stages. Start by getting people worried about the world ending. Then move on to a poster campaign. We've got to get them thinking in the back of their minds: *God, it might actually be going to happen*.'

This seemed reasonable. Fish, though, wasn't so sure. After all, he said, it wasn't the first time this threat had been issued. 'You don't want to look like a crank. Talking about the end of the world can lack credibility. And if people don't believe what you're saying, they won't respond. My feeling is you should use the idea of the world ending as a vehicle for a message people *would* accept.'

'Like?' said Jill.

'Like ... *Put your life in order*. We need to think, *What is the end benefit to everyone*? Well the end benefit is your life's in better shape, whether or not the world ends. You have a healthier, better life, a healthier, better world.' A sudden inspiration struck him. 'A signpost campaign. That would be quite interesting, signs hanging on lamp-posts...'

'Like the ones for Barratt Homes?' I ventured.

'But showing the way to heaven.'

'Yeah, I can see God selling heaven to them,' said Jill. 'Something like, he needs people to go to heaven to take part in his next project. Like he has a quota to fill.'

There was a feeling in the air that things were firming up. Fish pulled his jotting pad over.

'It's the temple thing,' he explained, sketching an end view of the Parthenon. 'If we dissect advertising, there's a big message on top that you're giving out to everyone. In this case that main message is that the world is going to end. But then you can have *supportive* campaigns fed into it.' He stroked in the pillars. 'These other campaigns tell people what they can do. For instance, one campaign I've always wanted to run is: BE NICE. Not for anyone in particular. Just BE NICE. It's relevant, especially in London. I think London creates more and more selfishness. People are career focused and it's hard to achieve a balance. That could be part of the campaign.'

He seemed quite moved by this. I nodded. 'Yes. I like that. Be nice – it says a lot.'

But another thought had struck him. 'A great place to advertise would be on planes. People getting out and going to their paradise. And that's another thing, isn't it? People will be seeking paradise. One of our aims is to say that paradise isn't over in Thailand or Mauritius. It's within.'

I was beginning to see what sort of inspirational vortex a creative might have to live in. We spent about an hour on these preliminaries, then got our diaries out.

'We'll write up a creative brief,' said Jill, 'using what we've discussed today. That will put the material in an ordered form so we can get the best creative work out of it. Normally we'd do some market research, but with the world ending we won't have time for that.'

'Research?'

'Among the target audience. We'd find out the most motivating way of telling them the world's going to end. And the answers would provide the hook for the brief – the one essential message we want to get through.'

Fish, meanwhile, had wandered onto a more philosophical track. 'It all comes down to selfishness again, though, doesn't it?' he said with a frown.

'You mean, people wanting to get into heaven?'

'Well, perhaps you just can't escape it, perhaps it's just the way the world is, perhaps it's circular, perhaps that's why...'

'But I thought,' I said, forgetting I was meant to be God, 'selfishness was the whole point of advertising. We're helping people gratify their desires.'

'Well,' interrupted Jill, brightly, 'shall we put a brief together? Then once you've approved the brief, the team can make some proposals and we can have a tissue meeting.'

This wasn't – as I first thought – a Kleenex binge for creatives whose carefully nurtured campaign ideas were being savaged by ungrateful clients. *Tissue* meant simply *unfinalized*.

We set a date, then I ran back to my parking meter, leaving the salvation of the universe in the hands of Britain's most famous advertising agency. They seemed pretty self-assured. But then self-assurance is the Saatchi & Saatchi style. You don't engrave the motto NOTHING IS IMPOSSIBLE into your black marble doorstep unless you mean business.

How do you tell someone the world's about to end?

The creative brief turned out to be a masterpiece of brevity, boiling an hour's discussion down to: *Get your life in order before it's too late.* In advertising-speak this is called a *single-minded proposition* – the one thing you really want to say. The agency's job now was to figure out a way of saying it.

On the day of the tissue meeting Fish had fallen ill and left the presentation to his team partner David Askwith. At that time Fish and Dave were looking after the accounts for Toyota and Club 18–30 – the latter assignment being much sought after since the creatives get to go out and sample the product. Following Dave through the Saatchi & Saatchi building, I discovered that most of the receptionists were called

Darlin'. He was relaxed, a dab hand with a teabag, and absolutely committed to the task. We collected Jill Simpson, found another conference room and went through the proposed campaign.

'The first problem you've got,' said Dave, 'is brand confusion. You can ask anyone in the world what the Devil looks like, and they'll say the same thing. The Devil's got his brand sorted out and you know what you're getting. But God's got lots of little brands under one umbrella – Buddha, Allah, Krishna. He needs pulling together.'

'You mean a logo...' I said.

'A logo,' said Dave. 'Exactly. A single, authoritative symbol. Now...' he took the top sheet off a large pile of papers '...this is how we're going to do it.'

Written in felt-tip were the words: PRIDE, WRATH, ENVY, LUST, GLUTTONY, GREED, SLOTH.

'The seven deadly sins,' said Dave. 'You see, almost any product or service appeals to one of those. So you need to advertise wherever people are buying them.'

I didn't quite see this. Dave pushed forward a second sheet.

'Condom wrappers,' he said. 'You've got ads on condom wrappers. These are for men's toilets. So the message reads: *I hope your girlfriend knows you're using this*, signed, *God*. Obviously that's lust. Here's another one – greed. This one's more of a stunt. There's someone ignoring a man sitting on the pavement asking for money. Then he sees the message on the billboard: *Do you really need that more than he does?* Signed, *God*. You're catching people as they've done something dodgy. Catching them red handed.'

'That man on the pavement's probably going to make a fortune,' observed Jill.

I asked Dave who he had in mind to run around sticking up billions of personalized messages.

'Well, this is no ordinary campaign,' Dave pointed out. 'We're assuming you'll want to use your supernatural powers.'

'Angels, then.'

'Is that a problem?'

'Not at all. I'm sure they'll enjoy the change.'

It made sense. The Angelic Host spends the world's last year on courier duty, running around leaving cryptic sin-specific notes on condom wrappers, cash machines, television, clouds – you name it. Every time a sinner's about to commit one of the seven deadlies, they flash up a made-to-measure warning. It's putting the conscience back into consciousness. What's the word? *Nagging* people.

'How do you think people will react?' I asked.

'It'll probably drive them absolutely mad,' replied Dave. 'But that's when you bring Doomsday in. You can use that oldest of advertising clichés, *A Once In a Lifetime Offer*. They've got however long until Doomsday to sort their lives out. Everything they've done until now is irrelevant. They've got so many days left to redress the balance.'

'And then...?'

Dave pulled down a final sheet. A checklist.

'Then we send them this. It tells you how many sins they've stopped committing. They fill it in themselves. If they score over 75 per cent, you let them into heaven.'

'And this goes into newspapers.'

'I think we'd direct mail it,' said Jill. 'Of course, we'd need a return address.'

'Yeah, so long as it's not Slough Industrial Estate,' added Dave. 'You've got to observe some basic standards.'

I admit I rather regretted the loss of BE NICE. On the other hand, the campaign was coherent, comprehensive and hard hitting – even if it left God pasting up a lot of his own posters. So, after giving the proposal the green light, I stepped back out over the Saatchi & Saatchi threshold feeling that, indeed, nothing was impossible if only you had the right pay-off line.

Still pretty chuffed with it all a few days later, I was bragging about the universal salvation plan to Steve Chalke, director of the Christian communications group Oasis Media. If *he* was God, I said, would he announce Doomsday with a Saatchi-&-Saatchi-style nagging campaign, or would he stick with the old sandwich boards? Steve pondered this for a moment, then replied, 'Actually, if I was God, I don't think I'd do any advertising at all. I'd just sneak up on them.'

It all depends what kind of God you are, I suppose.

SAATCHI & SAATCHI

80 CHARLOTTE STREET, LONDON W1A 1AQ. TEL: +44 171 636 5060. FAX: +44 171 637 8489.

TELEVISION SCRIPT

DATE	CLIENT	TITLE	WORD COUNT
19 October 1998	GOD	The end of the world	
JOB NUMBER	PRODUCT STAGE 1	LENGTH	SUBMISSION NUMBER

Not everyone believes in God. But they will. 365 days before the end of the world, God will simultaneously interrupt all live television and radio transmissions. This will be his message:

"I am God. Up until now, some of you have doubted my existence. Some of you have doubted the existence of Heaven and Hell. In exactly one year's time the world will end, and you will either be joining Me or joining Him. The choice is yours. If you care to look outside, I will give you a sign to prove I am all around you...."

At this point God turns daylight into night (or vice-versa), then turns it back.

"It's never too late to start being good. I'll see some of you very soon."

Agency: Saatchi and Saatchi. Creative team: Fish and David Aswith. Account Director: Jill Simpson. Stage 1: Script for God's simultaneous multi-channel TV commercial.

I saw that George! *God*

It's Not Really A Secret Affair Julian. *God*

Agency: Saatchi and Saatchi. Stage 2: The nagging billboard (examples A and B).

Agency: Saatchi and Saatchi. Stage 2: The nagging billboard (examples C and D).

HEAVEN: APPLICATION FORM

[Please complete in black ink]

1. Full name

2. Address/phone/e-mail where you can be reached between now and the end of the world

3. Religion (please tick):

[ ] Believe in one God
[ ] Believe in several Gods (please specify)
[ ] Believe in no Gods
[ ] Believe in fairies
[ ] Undecided

4. Reasons for application:

[ ] I am scared of going to hell
[ ] I tried to get into hell but my grades weren't good enough
[ ] At this point in my life I see heaven as sensible career move
[ ] I think there are better educational opportunities for my children

5. Please supply names and addresses of THREE referees, not including your mother. Please indicate if a referee is already dead. ALL REFERENCES WILL BE FOLLOWED UP.

6. Exemptions. I am claiming automatic entitlement to a place in heaven because:

[ ] I have a medical exemption certificate
[ ] I am under 16
[ ] I am receiving state benefits [please specify]
[ ] I was badly brought up
[ ] I am a recognised saint (please give date and name of presiding pope)

7. Which of the following statements best describes your current moral status:

[ ] I do whatever the hell I want to and screw everybody else
[ ] I do bad things but feel guilty about them
[ ] I do good things but feel guilty about them
[ ] I am perfect
[ ] I am a nervous wreck

8. If left alone in the presence of Morally Dubious Literature, would you:

[ ] Read it immediately
[ ] Check for video surveillance and then read it
[ ] Wish you could read it but not have the guts
[ ] Use it as lavatory paper

9. How many times have you turned the other cheek in the last seven days:

[ ] Never
[ ] Less than six times
[ ] Whenever I've had the chance
[ ] I have rheumatism

10. Which would you do to receive a free gift of ten million dollars:

[ ] Submit to gross humiliation on live TV
[ ] Undergo surgical nose-enlargement
[[Eat cockroaches every day for breakfast (without sugar)
[ ] None of the above

11. You are a government minister standing for "family values" and the media have just uncovered your illicit affair. How would you respond:

[ ] What I do in my private life is my own damn business
[ ] We had an improper relationship but no sex
[ ] Anybody like a cigar?
[ ] Okay, I resign.

12.............?

Agency: Saatchi and Saatchi. Stage 3: Direct mail application for heaven.

9

Get the Egg off your Face

There's not a lot of money in the end of the world. Unlike footballers, the sandwich-board men don't attract corporate sponsorship, nor have the broadcast rights been snapped up by Sky TV. But there is *some* money in it, and a proportion of these modest takings go to the bookmaker William Hill.

Admittedly, the amounts are small. When Matthew Dumbrell laid his bet for 11 August 1999, he only put down a pound. But as Hill's media relations manager Graham Sharpe points out, it's hard to envisage a bookmaker ever having to shell out on this one, so the annual £12.00 or so they make from Doomsday counts as solid profit. And it's no good trying to split theological hairs by distinguishing the end of the world from, say, the Second Coming of Christ.

'We once had a punter,' said Graham, 'who claimed the Second Coming had already happened. He even wrote to the Archbishop of Canterbury. He got a letter back from the Archbishop's office saying that, in the opinion of the Archbishop, when and if the Second Coming occurred it would coincide with the arrival of the four horsemen of the Apocalypse, which would equate to the end of the world and make it impossible to pay up.'

Nowadays, according to Graham, the Archbishop's role as arbitrator is routinely written into the bet – so presumably there's a fortune to be made by a bent cleric armed with a collection plate. Meanwhile, you can try your luck. The procedure's simple: you tell the bookmaker what you want to bet on, and he gives you written odds. They're pretty generous.

'Just this week we had a bet from a poet,' said Graham. 'He wanted to bet (a) that the Second Coming would be confirmed, and (b) that he himself would be confirmed as the Messiah. We offered him a million to one – the standard bet on the Second Coming. But frankly, for the end of the world you can have whatever you want. You can have a billion to one if you want. You can have a thousand billion million.'

I asked how the poet thought he was going to get the money.

Graham chuckled. 'He said I should make arrangements to take that amount with me so I could pay him.'

'What did he wager?'

'A pound.'

As you'd expect, a fair number of people who put money on the world ending do it so that they can wave a betting slip around in the bar. But some are deadly serious – and for these, predicting the end is a gamble of a different kind. It's one thing to survive the world ending; it's quite another to survive it *not* ending. What happens when you commit yourself, go on record with a date – and goof up? Do failed prophets, like failed priests, throw in the towel and become social workers? If your carefully calculated date turns out to be a lemon, how will you survive the ravages of post-prediction stress disorder? You'd better have a plan, because William Hill hasn't lost this wager yet.

Heading for the butter-and-honey star

It was time to do a bit more field research. Remembering that Marilyn Agee's date – 31 May 1998 – would come up before I'd finished the book, I decided to try to contact her. I imagined her as a tough, corporate type – city lawyer turned cult leader – so it didn't wholly surprise me when she failed to pick up the phone. When she replied to a desperate, last-ditch e-mail, however, I realized I'd got her quite wrong. She wrote:

> I appreciate your trying to contact me, but I am not home a lot of the time. I am in and out, in and out. We have Ed's doctor appointments (he went today), mine and his 92-year-old mother's. (For those we drive 90 to 140 miles. Did it last week and have to do that again tomorrow.) We go to the gym to Silver Sneaker exercise classes. We walk at the mall, trying to stay healthy (I am 69, Ed 74). We go to the Post Office just about every day. We go out to eat twice a day. I guess you see why I am not always here...

A prophet going to Silver Sneaker exercise classes? But with the end of the world approaching, and with so many reasons to think she'd picked the right date, there was clearly more on Marilyn's mind than keeping fit. She went on in some detail, drawing my attention to confirmatory signs. Had I noticed that it had snowed five inches in Jerusalem before spring? Also in New York? In fact, in the mountains of southern California it was still snowing. She quoted me Proverbs 25:13: *As the cold of snow in the time of harvest, so is a faithful messenger to them that send him.* 'The Rapture is the wheat harvest,' she said. 'This unseasonable snow makes me wonder.'

What interested me – in fact I found it reassuring – was that Marilyn's passion about the Rapture hadn't stopped her living a normal life. She wasn't all bluster and self-assertion. Unlike the more aggressive prophets, she'd step out from behind the barricades and chat. In my next e-mail I asked her if she had a following. She said no. God had led her to study prophecy, and to share her findings she'd written three books and set up a web-page called *Bible Prophecy Corner*. But she didn't regard herself as a leader, nor did she have a group around her.

And how certain was she that the world was ending? Trying to make clear the costs involved, I asked if she'd consider – say – blowing her savings on a holiday before the date came. Here again, though, Marilyn Agee had her feet firmly on the ground. 'I have no savings to blow,' she returned. 'We have not had a vacation for so long that I can't remember when we did. My concern is to keep a roof over our heads and food in our mouths. As to the certainty of the date, I am not a prophet and cannot say, "Thus saith the Lord." I merely say that this is how it looks to me. However, personally, I expect the Rapture on Pentecost, May 31, 1998. All the signs seem to converge on 1998, 5758 on the Jewish Calendar.'

If we all turned out to be still here on 1 June 1998, therefore, Marilyn could not be accused of misrepresenting God – only of being a poor scholar. Nevertheless, she'd clearly invested her reputation in being right and was looking forward to the Rapture as other people might look forward to a holiday in the Maldives. Come the morning of 1 June, she said, she'd be up there 'attending the assembly in Heaven'.

Marilyn has seen heaven already, albeit from a distance. In fact, heaven – the 'butter-and-honey star' – is visible from her back garden. It's the planet Saturn. Had pictures from space probes, I wondered, done anything to challenge this belief? But Marilyn saw NASA as a staunch ally. 'Heaven has golden clouds and seven rings around it,' she replied. 'The Voyager expeditions proved that Saturn has seven rings. We already knew that it had golden clouds, but the pictures gave details not seen before.'

And what, I asked finally, did her husband Ed feel about her predictions? I wondered if Ed was quite as keen for the world to end as she was. But Ed seemed to be up there waving the pom-poms. 'He hopes I'm right,' said Marilyn, 'and says that all the signs look like it will happen at that time.'

That was early April. There were seven weeks to go.

Mrs Keech takes it on the chin

Meanwhile, I wanted to find out what had happened to others in Marilyn's position. Studies of this are comparatively rare, and one of the most thorough – as well as the most entertaining – is still Leon Festinger's *When Prophecy Fails*.[1]

Back in the 1950s Festinger had discovered a Mrs Keech, who expected to be rescued from a coming cataclysm by spacemen in flying saucers. Not to miss an opportunity like this, Festinger and his colleagues set up an intricate programme of surveillance and infiltration, which climaxed on 23 December, when the spacemen gave orders for a rendezvous. Mrs Keech's group, the message said, was to assemble on the pavement outside her home at 6.00 p.m., Christmas Eve, and sing Christmas carols. The spacemen would land in a flying saucer.

Thus far, it has to be said, the spacemen hadn't proved very reliable. Secret meetings promised for 17 and 21 December had both ended in disappointment. Also, just the previous afternoon a long message had instructed Mrs Keech to sit with her finger pointing at a tape deck so that she could transmit to it 'a pretty song which has been sung by the boys' glee club of the Losoloes'. Played back, the tape turned out to be blank.

This last communication, however, promised a defining moment. Not only were the faithful to await the visitation in a public place –

they were to invite the press. Notwithstanding past failures, then, Christmas Eve was awaited with real expectation, and when the Keech party stepped onto the street at 6 o'clock there were 200 people standing outside to watch.

Alas, once again the spacemen stood them up. By 6.20 the party had retreated indoors again – and not for sherry and mince pies. It was shortly afterwards that the phone rang and Mrs Keech's sidekick, Dr Armstrong, found himself talking to a reporter. Festinger details the conversation like this:

NEWSMAN: Dr Armstrong, I wanted to talk to you with reference to this business about – you know – your calling the paper to say you were going to be picked up at 6 o'clock this evening. Ahh, I wanted to find out exactly what happened ... Didn't you say they sent a message that you should be packed and waiting at 6 p.m., Christmas Eve?

DR ARMSTRONG: No.

NEWSMAN: No? No, I'm sorry, sir. Weren't the spacemen supposed to pick you up at 6 p.m.?

DR ARMSTRONG: Well, there was a spaceman in the crowd with a helmet on and a white gown and what-not.

NEWSMAN: There was a spaceman in the crowd?

DR ARMSTRONG: Well, it was a little hard to tell, but of course at the last when we broke up, why there was very evidently a spaceman there because he had his space helmet on and he had a big white gown on.

NEWSMAN: Oh, the spacemen were there?

DR ARMSTRONG: Well, there was one there.

NEWSMAN: One spaceman there. And what did he say? Did you talk to him?

DR ARMSTRONG: No, I didn't talk to him.
NEWSMAN: Did you say you were going to be picked up by the spacemen?
DR ARMSTRONG: No.
NEWSMAN: Well, what were you waiting out in the street for, singing carols?
DR ARMSTRONG: Well, we went out to sing Christmas carols.
NEWSMAN: Oh, you just went out to sing Christmas carols?
DR ARMSTRONG: Well, and if anything happened, well, that's all right, you know. We live from one minute to another. Some very strange things have happened to us and–
NEWSMAN: But didn't you hope to be picked up by the spacemen? As I understand it–
DR ARMSTRONG: We were willing.
NEWSMAN: You were willing to be picked up by the spacemen. But didn't you expect them to pick you up? As I understand it, you said you expected them to come but they might change their minds, that they're unpredictable. Is that correct?
DR ARMSTRONG: Well, ahh, I didn't see the paper, what was actually printed in the paper.
NEWSMAN: Well, no, but isn't that what you said?
DR ARMSTRONG: We had some instructions to pass on the news, ya, that the spacemen possibly would pick us up...
NEWSMAN: Uhuh. Well, how do you account for the fact that they didn't pick you up?
DR ARMSTRONG: Well, as I told one of the other news boys, I didn't think a spaceman would feel very welcome in that crowd.[2]

I think the word here is *squirming*. In the language of the experts, Dr Armstrong had just experienced a *disconfirmation* of his belief, and was now being required to explain why it had happened. He'd claimed the spacemen would appear and rescue the group from the coming cataclysm. The spacemen hadn't appeared. How were belief and reality to be reconciled?

Confronting this question is an occupational hazard in the prediction business. Dr Armstrong had to think on his feet. It's advisable, though, to have your arguments prepared – so if you really *have* to put a date on it, think through right now how you'll explain a failure when the media come knocking on your door. The main options seem to be these:

1. **Ditch your religion.** You paid good money for it, and it broke – so take it back to the shop and demand your money back. You may think this is obvious. Surprisingly, though, people who buy a religion don't often part with it. Like dogs, religions are for life. Even as self-evidently daft a belief as Mrs Keech's (sorry, I know that's unprofessional) maintained a grip on her followers. In fact, only two of the group dropped out after the saucer failed to show up. The other nine, reports Festinger, 'emerged from the period of disconfirmation and its aftermath with their faith firm, unshaken, and lasting.'
2. **Bite the bullet.** Let's face it, you've put other people to a lot of inconvenience, so a word of apology won't go amiss. Or, if not an apology, then at least an admission that it was your fault. Following God's failure to address the nation as promised on America's Channel 18, for instance, sect leader Hon-Ming Chen, a former university lecturer, rather touchingly withdrew his prediction that the world would end at 10.00 a.m. on 31 March 1998. 'Since God's appearance on television has not been realized, you can take what we have preached as nonsense. I would rather you

don't believe what I say any more.'[3] If only governments would say that about economic policy.

3. **Blame God.** In the nicest possible way, of course. In fact, this has been the old faithful of failed prophets in every generation. God said he was going to end the world, but hey (isn't he just a wild and crazy guy?), he didn't mean it – what he *really* wanted to do was *test our faith*. After a little thought, this was the position Mr Chen came around to. 'God has communicated to me,' he said later, 'that if I want to take the responsibility of preaching his gospel, I have to have the courage to face the scoffing and laughter of people.' Probably true. Watch out for your credibility, though.

4. **Blame your calculator.** It wasn't you. It wasn't the concept. It was just some unidentified glitch in the maths. So hang in there, folks, while we check the sums again. Whatever you do, don't touch that dial. We'll be back right after these messages ... A note to remember, though: if you don't want to get your fingers burned twice, you should go for something less specific. 'Soon' is a recommended choice.

5. **Blame the weather.** Or, if not the weather exactly, then some other circumstance beyond your (or God's) control. In effect, this was one of the first ideas to pop into Dr Armstrong's head after the carol-singing crisis. The spacemen hadn't come, he said, because the public they'd insisted on notifying had inconsiderately turned up to watch. Later he elaborated on this, explaining that the spacemen had stayed away so as to prevent a riot. Or perhaps – given that this was Christmas Eve – they were out in their flying saucer helping Santa Claus?

6. **Be brazen.** Harold Camping of the Christian broadcasting organization *Family Radio* scrutinized the Bible's genealogical record and concluded that the Second Coming would happen in 1994. He even wrote a book about it. When the prediction flopped and the

press came round to thumb their noses at him, Camping did a swift about-turn. He'd guessed wrong – so what? But because the media had hyped his book, millions of people all around the world had heard about the Second Coming, and contributions to his ministry had quadrupled.[4] You've got to admit, it takes guts.

7. **Redefine your terms.** Quite subtle, this one. True, you didn't actually see the world end. True, we're all still here instead of harping in heaven or hollering in hell. But that's only how it *looks*. Really the world did end, exactly on schedule, but in a *spiritual* sense. This is much the viewpoint adopted by the Seventh Day Adventists. After William Miller three times failed to get the date right in 1843/44 (an event later dubbed the Great Disappointment) he went for Options 2 and 1, telling his estimated 50,000 supporters, 'I confess my error and acknowledge my disappointment.' But they'd have none of it. The position many finally adopted was put forward by Hiram Edson, an Adventist leader from New York State, who used Paul's letter to the Hebrews to show that Miller had been right about the date, but wrong about what the date *meant*. The year 1843 marked the point, not when Christ came *out* of the heavenly sanctuary to return to earth, but when he *entered* it. So that's all right then.

Wrong again (and again): the Jehovah's Witnesses

The Jehovah's Witnesses are the undisputed champions in the business of getting dates wrong – their critics accusing them of having fallen off the wagon in this regard on at least seven different occasions. As you might expect, the history of the movement has been one of struggle with Option 4, apparent failures sometimes being covered with forays into Option 7. Among the key early dates were 1873, identified by the movement's founder Charles Russell as the beginning of the thousand-year reign of Christ,[5] and 1914, when 'the battle of the great day of the Almighty' (Revelation 16:14) was expected to result in the 'complete overthrow of the earth's present rulership'.[6]

No tangible change occurred on either occasion, however. When another disappointment was clocked up in 1925, Russell's successor Joseph Rutherford famously admitted, 'I made an ass of myself,' and after Rutherford died in 1942 it was announced that the date of Adam's creation used during the Russell and Rutherford presidencies was out by some 100 years. For a quarter of a century prediction fell from favour. Then, in 1966, a book entitled *Life Everlasting in Freedom of the Sons of God* declared that 'the seventh period of a thousand years of human history will begin in the fall of 1975'.[7]

Of course, there is some argument over what constitutes an *official* prophecy. Perhaps mindful of past errors, the leadership was reluctant to link 1975 with explicit end-time events. On the other hand, as 1975 established itself as a year of prophetic significance, Jehovah's Witnesses saw a dramatic increase in conversions (see the graph overleaf). The lesson seemed clear: prediction was good for business.[8]

With 1975 bearing down on them, then, the leadership equivocated. At no point was an out-and-out claim made that 1975 would bring the end of the current world order. Nevertheless, official publications declared it 'appropriate ... for Jehovah God to make of this coming seventh period of a thousand years a Sabbath period of rest and release...'[9] Whatever more cautionary notes were sounded, it must have been hard to read some official publications without detecting in them subtle references to 1975. 'Within a few years at most,' said one writer, 'the final parts of Bible prophecy relative to these "last days" will undergo fulfilment ... what grand days are just ahead!'[10] And in a magazine that went only to members, the example of 'brothers selling their homes and property ... to finish out the rest of their days in this old system in

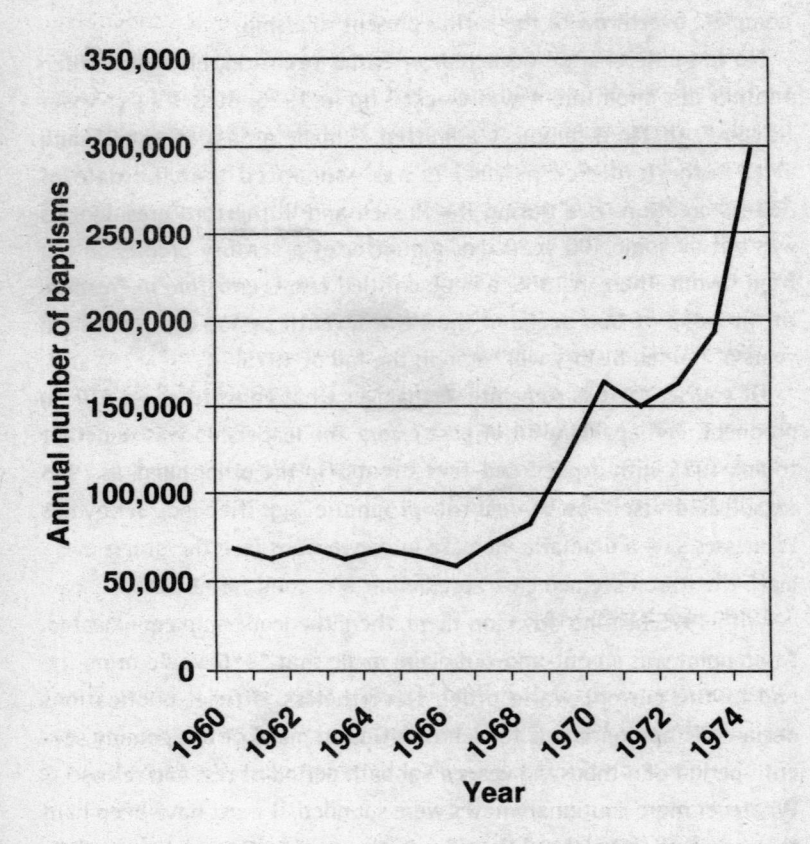

Baptisms in the Jehovah's Witnesses. 1975 began to be highlighted as a possible date for the end of the world in 1966.

the pioneer service' was commended as 'a fine way to spend the short time remaining before the wicked world's end'.[11]

Well, 1975 came and went. Initial reactions were guarded. 'If anyone has been disappointed,' said *The Watchtower* in 1976, 'he should concentrate on adjusting his viewpoint, seeing that it was not the word of God that failed or deceived him ... but that his own understanding was based on wrong premises.'[12] Four years later, however, they were clarifying this in what virtually amounted to a retraction: 'In saying "anyone," *The Watchtower* included all disappointed ones of Jehovah's Witnesses, hence including *persons having to do with the publication of the information* that contributed to the build-up of hopes centered on that date.'[13]

When 1994 arrived, comment on it as the conclusion of an 80-year biblical generation was muted. Finally, in 1995 *The Watchtower* declared, 'We do not need to know the exact timing of events. Rather our focus must be on being watchful, cultivating strong faith, and keeping busy in Jehovah's service.'[14]

Given up guessing?

Other prophecy-wonkers greet this declaration with a sly wink. They'll be back, they say. No one kicks the prediction habit overnight, they say. It's old dogs and new tricks, they say. You might as well teach koalas to limbo-dance.

So was 1975 positively the last guess for the Jehovah's Witnesses? To find out, I really had only one option – to go and see them. Anyone who's been buttonholed on the doorstep may feel that this was unduly reckless. Certainly in my father's circles the 'JWs' were seen as a kind of Red Army elite corps, brainwashed in mass training sessions and stuffed with so many rote arguments for their cause that only the most seasoned Bible student should consider taking them on in single combat.

I have to say, though, that Paul Gillies, press officer for JWUK, did not strike me as an agent of the devil. He did not betray a gruff, Muscovite accent. Nor could I see a limp, red, serrated tail humped over the back of his chair. He looked, in fact, like the sort of pleasant, middle-aged bloke you'd meet on the golf links. As we walked across the vast and empty lobby of the organization's HQ in north London, I started by asking him what he thought the end of the world would be like.

'Oh, dramatic,' he said. 'The Bible describes it as a great tribulation such as mankind has never seen before, nor will ever see again. A vast, vast change. The comparison in the Bible is with the flood of Noah's day, which ended a whole world system.'

He was very definite about Bible chronology pointing to 1914 as the beginning of the last days. When I mentioned past mistakes, however, he looked a little cagey. 'Ever since that was clear to us,' he explained, 'there has been an element of *speculation* about the timing of the actual intervention by Jesus Christ and the angels. When a date has coincided with specific chronology in the Bible, we've said that would be an "appropriate" time.'

'Appropriate' or not, however, God hadn't seemed to take the hint. Had they now abandoned the idea of an imminent end? Mr Gillies chose his words carefully.

'We view these things as *premature expectations*, rather than meaning the end is not coming at all. Premature expectations rather than false prophecies. It's rather like if a very close friend said he was going to arrive at the airport on such and such a date, but hadn't given a time or a flight number. You know this person to be truthful, so you might go down to the airport early in the morning and watch all the flights coming in. You'd have speculations and disappointments, but you'd stay ready and on the watch.'

This had the well-tried feel of official explanation. I don't think Mr Gillies meant (as the analogy seemed to imply) that sooner or later midnight would come and the passenger would have to be given up for lost. But either way, I said, wasn't there a human cost to this vigil? After all, it's hard both to expect and *not* expect at the same time. Naturally you pin your hopes on the next flight being the one.

'I think that's a fair question,' returned Mr Gillies. And here for a moment the weight of his responsibility as press officer seemed to lift a little and let through a glimmer of his own experience – for he was old enough to have lived through 1975. 'It has to be said,' he acknowledged, 'that some have been disappointed and have gone away from the congregations because they felt they were misled. All of us who were on the watch, and were perhaps in expectation to some degree, are disappointed because we wanted to see an end to suffering, famines and war. We've learned lessons. We've learned to listen more closely to what the Bible says. When the Bible doesn't say something specifically we'd rather stay with what the Bible does say, and not affect people's lives by trying to speculate.'

So 1975 was indeed the last of the 'appropriate times'. Which leaves Jehovah's Witnesses exactly where?

'Well, we're not just focused on prophecy,' underlined Mr Gillies. 'We're focused on environmental issues. We're focused on family life. We're focused on moral standards. In the last three years we've printed upwards of 80 articles on the environment. Once you've formed an organization, you have to enlarge on the teaching. You've got to show people how to live together. We have community responsibilities for things like paying the taxes that keep society going. You can't just say, well it's all coming to an end, therefore we have no interest in it.'

Even Jehovah's Witnesses, therefore, seem to have flirted with the accommodation to permanence. According to Paul Gillies, this movement born amid concrete assertions of the world's end 'remains convinced the end will come according to God's timetable'. Yet the emphasis is no longer on 'a certain date ahead', but on the practicalities of day-to-day living.[15]

Much the same happened to the early Christian Church. Even Jesus, it seems, didn't anticipate much more than a shower and a change of clothes before going back down to gather his elect. But the years rolled by; the demands of everyday life became ever more pressing. Inevitably, as evening wears on, the people at the arrivals gate glance at the clock and wonder – in the event of the flight being delayed – where they might go to catch a few hours' sleep.

What happened to Marilyn Agee

I'd meant to take a winter coat out with me on 31 May, just in case I was raptured and taken to Saturn. The temperature's pretty low on Saturn – something Mrs Agee doesn't concern herself with. You also can't breathe. Anyway, it proved of no consequence, since I woke up next morning still very much on earth. Afraid it would look predatory to e-mail her straight away, I left it until the end of the week and then sent her some gentle and polite questions:

1. At what point did you realize 31 May wasn't the day?
2. Has that knowledge shaken your faith, or your belief that the end can be predicted?
3. Do you know why that date was wrong?
4. What will be your priorities now?

The replies were terse:

1. When it passed.
2. No to both.
3. I think it was the Jewish Calendar I was going by.
4. Right now I expect the Rapture to happen this weekend, on the Greek Orthodox Pentecost.

Nothing could shake her faith, she said. She was excited to find out about the other calendar, which she hadn't known about before. 'We have snow in the time of harvest,' she added. 'Have you seen the weather reports? Time is short. Be READY for the Rapture.' Option 4, then, to kick off with.

It was midsummer before I contacted her again. By now, things had indeed changed – but not in the way she'd expected. Her reply came in on 18 August:

Hi:
I am well. My husband had a heart attack and 5-bypass open-heart surgery. I have him home now and am very busy taking care of him. I had prayed that he would be with me until the Rapture, and this must be the only way it was going to happen. I praise the Lord for making all things work together for good for those that love Him. I am hoping for the Rapture soon, before summer is over, maybe September 20, the Eve of the Feast of Trumpets. If not then, before the Tribulation for sure.

I think we are probably being tested to see who stays awake and who falls asleep. Jesus told Peter that Satan desired to sift him as wheat. We are wheat, and this may be our sifting. If it is, I intend to stay in the sieve. I am in this for the long haul if that is what it takes. 'Blessed are those servants, whom the Lord when he cometh shall find watching' (Luke 12:37).

In His love, Marilyn Agee

So: Option 4, now supplemented by Option 3.

At least she's candid about it – but then, maybe candour comes more easily when you're working alone than it does when you're a multi-million-member organization. It also softens the blow a little if you're not surrounded by a bunch of people who've relied on you getting the prediction right. Marilyn gave it her best shot. She was fairly beaten, and she doesn't argue. You have to respect her for that.

10

Snack-sized Armageddons

If you want to see Doomsday, go to the Tate Gallery in London – it's in Room 6. Turn left at the Rotunda, take 30 paces towards a naked man throttling a viper, and you'll see it on the wall ahead of you: John Martin's *The Great Day of His Wrath*. It's exactly what it says on the tin: the world in the act of ending. Near the bottom tiny, naked figures slither into a black abyss, while above them, in towering perspective, the skies crack open and bits of mountain the size of skyscrapers lurch free and prepare to tumble. It's the disaster-movie version of the end of time, rendered in the best medium available to a Victorian artist; it's God coming back to break up the party.

But Doomsday is available in plenty of versions that don't entail the wholesale destruction of the universe. Most of our current so-called Doomsday scenarios, in fact, don't feature God at all, and in cosmic terms are pretty hole-in-the-corner affairs. The planet could outlive us. So could fruit flies. So could crisp packets. We could vanish off the map before anyone's noticed we're here. And who knows what apparently insignificant tremors might flick us off the end of the evolutionary plank?

DOOMSDAY

Hey...life goes on.

Agency: Rapier. Copywriter: Simon Welsh. Art Director: Tom Geens. 'Client': The Dino Followers.

SNACK-SIZED ARMAGEDDONS

The dinosaurs: a sober warning

In the competition to survive, the dinosaurs were the fittest of the fit. They pumped iron. They swaggered around for the best part of 100 million years and absolutely no one could challenge them. They were at the top of every food chain. Nothing in geological history has ever grown bigger than a dinosaur and still been able to walk. If evolution is a surfboard, the dinosaurs rode the biggest rollers and stayed on them longer than anybody else. And yet the one thing every four-year-old kid knows about dinosaurs is that they're extinct. In the blink of an eye (10 million years is a blink in geological terms) they were history.

What did for the dinosaurs? Well, no one's entirely sure. Possibly they'd been hogging the ball for long enough and God thought it was time for someone else to have a go. In which case we're back to prophecy-wonking and the book of Revelation. But if dinosaurs died of *natural causes*, what can we learn from them? It all depends, of course, which dead-dino theory you favour. Here, anyway, are some of the main contenders, and what seem to me to be the relevant implications for us:

1. Mammals get partial to dinosaur egg on toast

Described by some as 'mammalian chauvinism', this theory suggests that fat, old, lumbering dinosaurs just couldn't lay eggs fast enough to stop small, nimble, hairy mammals carrying them off for tea. Appealing though this is, it fails to account for the simultaneous extinction of many *marine* species (unless the small, hairy mammals were also very good swimmers). Given that dinosaurs for the most part laid their eggs on the ground, the *accidental-egg-trampling* theory seems to have more going for it.

LESSON: Try not to lay eggs. Don't leave your child unattended in a place where small, hairy mammals might make off with it.

2. The death planet cometh (every 26 million years)

Calculating that mass extinctions have occurred at roughly 26-million-year intervals (the most recent being 12 million years ago, in the mid-Miocene), some theorists have suggested that there is an undiscovered tenth planet (they called it Nemesis) whose orbit is so eccentric that it only comes near the rest of the solar system every 26 million years. Its arrival is bad news because it disturbs the Oort cometary cloud at the outermost fringes of the system, sending debris hurtling towards the earth. Critics point out that Nemesis has yet to be found and that, anyway, the 26-million-year cycle only works for three of the eight known mass extinctions.

LESSON: If you're still around in the year AD 14000000, keep the family indoors as much as possible.

3. Nearby supernova turns earth into sunbed

A neighbouring supernova emits a wave of lethal X-rays, and dinosaurs are too slow to take cover and/or too big to squeeze into nearby caves. Notwithstanding the dinosaurs' current resemblance to X-ray film, this is an unsatisfactory explanation, since mammals aren't known to have been more radiation-proof than the dinosaurs, and the extinguished marine species ought to have been protected by the water.

LESSON: Always carry a lead umbrella. If your bones become unexpectedly visible, put it up fast.

4. Climate gets hot/cold flushes

A number of theories suggest that the dinosaurs were wrong-footed by sudden climate change. On one reckoning the solar system plunged into a cloud of galactic dust, fuelling the sun, increasing temperatures and rendering male dinos sterile. On another, whatever caused the 150-million-year heatwave of the Jurassic and Cretaceous periods suddenly conked out, with the result that northerly dinosaurs had to invent double-glazing or die. For some reason they chose the latter.

LESSON: Don't trust weather forecasts. Keep Viagra and a spare sweater in your bag.

5. Dino docs lack flu jabs

Palaeontologist Dr Robert T. Bakker has suggested that a fall in global sea levels at the close of the Cretaceous period opened up new land bridges between the continents. Dinosaurs, being biggest and dumbest, were the first to cross, and the first to die as a result of contact with unfamiliar parasites and diseases. Problems include plate tectonics and the determination of small animals. For example, opossums – not known for breaking land speed records – have still managed to move from South to North America via Panama.

LESSON: Avoid crossing land bridges to populate new continents. If you must, then make sure you have the right booster injections before you go.

6. Small, hairy aliens come on safari

This is my personal favourite – in fact, I thought it up all by myself. Around 64400000 BC we came under the control of the Intergalactic Tourist Board and were licensed out to developers. Warm volcanic seas drew the tourists in droves, many of whom spent an afternoon out popping the wildlife. Think – have you ever seen a dinosaur that looked as if it had died in its bed? Come to that, have you ever seen a dinosaur still with its tusks? Of course not – conclusive proof that T-Rex and pals were hunted for ivory. And in case you're wondering about the marine extinctions, don't forget that these people had to eat. Dead ammonites didn't just sink to the bottom of the ocean. They were trawled up, boiled, smothered in garlic sauce and eaten *al fresco* at beach parties.

LESSON: Kill Martians on sight. See Chapter 7.

Big things that fall from the sky

The sexiest theory about dinosaurs right now is the one involving asteroids. 66.4 million years ago our luck gave out on the cosmic coconut shy and we got hit by something six and a half miles across. The impact made H-bombs look like a chip-pan fire. Tsunamis and persistent cloud (of the kind still seen in western Scotland) made the world a miserable place to live for the best part of a decade, and afterwards vast tracts of empty ecosytem were up for sale. Hardly believing their luck, the mammals, until then just evolutionary also-rans, moved in and took over. The dinosaurs had gone. All that remained of them were a few strands of mosquito-sucked DNA trapped in blobs of amber.

Surprisingly, the notion that humans might take a hit too goes back to 1883, when the American novelist, politician and social reformer Ignatius Donnelly published a book called *Ragnorak, The Age of Fire and Gravel*. Certain soil substrata, suggested Donnelly, could be explained only by the effects of a cometary near-miss. And it was only a matter of time before the rogue ball of ice and dirt came back to finish us off. He wrote the entire work of 450 pages in just seven weeks, saying afterwards, 'I could not rest until I had written it out and then the great dread of my soul was that some accident would destroy the single copy and the world would lose a revelation.' Clearly, then, he had a computer.

Were Donnelly's fears well founded? There is, of course, only one authority worth consulting about comets or anything else in space, and that is Patrick Moore. The world's favourite astronomer has a cottage in the village of Selsey, West Sussex, to which the word 'rambling' naturally attaches itself. He started presenting the BBC's *Sky at Night* long before I was born. Initially they gave him just five minutes for the show, and he responded by frowning at the camera and talking like a machine gun.

Only Patrick Moore would have three telescopes in his back garden, and only Patrick Moore could construct movable canopies for them using, it appears, only old railway track, a bicycle and an assortment of garage doors. He insisted that I bring my children along. We duly inspected the hardware outside and retired to the living room where he keeps his glockenspiels and piano. On the larger glockenspiel a notice said: *No you CAN'T put your mug down here*. Obediently I held my mug on my lap.

'Let's face it, we *could* be hit by a meteoroid, an asteroid, or a comet,' he said in answer to my query. 'We've been hit twice in the twentieth century. Once in 1908, once in 1927. Both by a smallish meteoroid. One wiped out a wide area of south Siberia. The other caused a crater near Vladivostok. There are impact craters on earth. Very famous one, of course, in Arizona.'

Two in one century seemed rather close for comfort. Was it likely that we'd get hit again?

'The chances of a major strike in the near future,' Patrick Moore assured me, 'are astonishingly small. But if something a mile wide hit us it would cause global devastation, no doubt about it. Might even wipe out civilization. Probably it would rupture the earth's crust, causing global earthquakes and widespread tsunami. It would throw a tremendous amount of dust and debris into the atmosphere. And that could block out the sunlight and cause a complete global change in the climate. Certainly, if a thing 500 feet across fell on Manchester there wouldn't be much left of Selsey. Tea satisfactory, by the way?'

The tea was fine. I asked how much warning we'd be given, just in case we could get out of the way. But Patrick Moore was shaking his head.

'We might not know till it had passed us. Most of these near-earth asteroids – we call them NEAs – aren't seen till they're past their closest approach. We might have no warning at all.'

'Not even you with your telescopes?'

'Nope,' he said triumphantly. 'Not even me. They're faint. They're unpredictable. They're slow moving. If you don't have the right background you won't find it until it's past.'

He was unimpressed by Spacewatch – a project set up recently to scan the skies for incoming disasters – and positively scornful of the efforts a body like the UN might make to coordinate a response. 'Also,' he said, 'if you did see one coming, what would you do? You certainly couldn't break it up, because if you did you'd be peppered with shrapnel. The only thing you might be able to do is explode a nuclear device very near it, or on the surface, and divert it. That, I suppose, would be a possibility, but it's jolly dicey.'

Finally I came to the matter of personal survival. 'Suppose we had some warning,' I said, 'and suppose we knew a major comet strike was about to occur. What advice would you give to ordinary people? What should we do?'

A cheerful smile broke out on Patrick Moore's face. 'Repeat after me,' he replied. '*Our Father, which art in heaven...*'

In a nutshell, then, we're all doomed. Although he didn't subscribe to the theory that dinosaurs were wiped out by comet impact – the iridium spike associated with the dinosaur extinction being, he said, conspicuously absent in earlier, larger mass extinctions like that of the Permian period. I couldn't leave, though, without asking Patrick Moore about Saturn. Marilyn Agee, remember, claimed that heaven was located on the planet – a belief that data from space probes had done nothing to dent. I asked Patrick Moore if he regarded this idea as plausible.

He replied with great seriousness, 'I think it would be difficult. After all, it has no solid surface. There's a great deal of hydrogen and helium in the atmosphere, and nothing to stand on. So I'd have to say I think it's very unlikely.' Then he gave a sudden, uproarious laugh and added, 'You know the Ethereal Society are very fond of Saturn. The Ethereal Society are great fun. I wrote a book a while ago, now sadly out of print...'

He fetched a copy of *Can You Speak Venusian?* and handed it to me, open at the appropriate paragraph. He'd been interviewing the Society secretary about their belief in the Interplanetary Parliament. I quoted him aloud: 'I asked Mr Robinson what the Saturnians looked like, and he replied that by this stage in its evolution a being has gained such a status that it can be seen in its entirety, that is to say, an ovoid shape – a great incandescent egg perhaps 40 feet tall. I commented that the Saturnians seemed to be extremely large balls ...'

At this point the author cut in. 'And he replied, "Yes, they're complete balls"!' He guffawed, then added with a twinkle, 'It was a difficult moment.'

Told you s☮

Agency: WWAV Rapp Collins. Copywriter: Jeremy Golding. Art Director: Yuk Man.

How to finance your asteroid disaster

Just as people bet on the end of time, so they try to lay bets on various lesser kinds of disaster: comets, asteroids, earthquakes, hurricanes.

'We often get requests for them,' said Graham Sharpe of William Hill. 'But we point out to people, "If this bet wins, probably 10,000 people will have lost their lives. Would you be happy with that on your conscience?"'

'What do they say?'

'Usually they say yes. But we don't accept bets like that. There are plenty of things to bet on that don't involve doom and gloom.'

I suggested to him that – technically speaking – bets like Matthew Dumbrell's implied a kind of mass homicide. But Graham seemed relaxed about this. 'We figure the end of the world means nobody's going to be around to complain about us doing it.'

Stock market collapses were also out, though not because ex-millionaires were in the habit of launching themselves from upper windows in Manhattan. 'We just lack the specialist knowledge,' said Graham.

No sudden fortunes to be made from falling rocks, then. What, though, did the insurance industry make of the threat? If you couldn't speculate on disaster, you might at least be able to cover yourself for losses. On a whim I called Lloyd's Insurance Market and was put through to a man called Richard Keeling, a director of the Amlin group. He told me that asteroid strikes are frequently specified in insurance cover for communications satellites, though the chances of one being hit, or even winged, are very remote. Similar calculations govern surface strikes.

'I read somewhere that you have far less chance of being killed by an asteroid than you do by flying in planes. Life may get wiped out by an asteroid, but on average that only happens every so many million years. So statistically it's correct.'

Like bookmakers, insurers can heave a sigh of relief if an asteroid strike results in total wipe-out. The real nightmare is a limited impact – still being around, in other words, to pay out cripplingly whopping claims. I asked Richard Keeling what we should do to cover ourselves. To which the answer is: probably nothing. In fact, it's likely that your existing policy already covers you – by default.

'An all-risk policy,' he said, 'means *all-risk* unless you specifically exclude something. If you haven't excluded it, it will be covered. Of course, there are millions of policies, and millions of different interpretations of policies, but there are quite a lot that would respond. Your life policy would respond, I think. Your personal accident policy probably would respond. But I'm sure there are other coverages where the insurers would say no, this is not covered. It's difficult to be definitive, but I think on a broad sweep the probability is that there are a lot of insurance assets at risk on a strike.'

The Spengler Hypothesis: tomorrow we wilt

Of course, those more recent dinosaurs, the Romans, didn't need an asteroid to kick them into touch. They did it all by themselves. And the lingering extinction of the world's greatest empire has fuelled a wholly different line of theorizing about the way worlds end. The most celebrated of them – if not the best known – came from a German of the early twentieth century called Oswald Spengler. Shpengler (as he pronounced himself) took a long, hard look at the way civilizations behave, and concluded that you can't keep a civilization alive indefinitely any more than you can keep a beetle alive in a jam jar. Never mind asteroids and avenging gods: the typical civilization will leaf, bloom and wither entirely of its own accord. Hormone replacement is useless. Obsolescence is built in. Unsurprisingly, Spengler entitled his magnum opus *The Decline of the West*.

To check whether or not global civilization was lurching into a precipitous decline, I made an appointment with my local Member of Parliament, Simon Hughes. He's Health and London Spokesman for the British Liberal-Democratic Party, and also a disconcertingly Nice Bloke. We met for coffee at one of the canteens where perspiring politicians get their breath back between debates. They've hung Baroness Thatcher at one end of the room, and Lord Wilson at the other. We sat in the blue corner – under Mrs T.'s unforgiving gaze – and kept our voices down.

I asked Simon where he thought we might be by the end of the next century.

'In political terms, I think we'll be living in a world with continental governments', he said. 'The nation states will be small pieces in the jigsaw. And there'll be a much stronger UN organization which is seen to be much more relevant, the place where disputes are taken for resolution.'

Well, at least we're all still here. Meanwhile, did he feel upbeat or slightly depressed at the way things were going?

It was clearly a close race. 'Overall we're healthier than we were. Also better educated, which is an insurance policy against foolishness – or it should be. On the other hand, we're always at risk of messing up our ecology, and there's still a lot of inequality around, both within countries and between them. So there are reasons for optimism, and reasons for pessimism.' He grinned. 'Meanwhile, in the absence of a definite conclusion, I remain optimistic.'

For Simon Hughes, then, the glass of history is half full, not half empty. But that's a long way from being home and dry. If a person could do just one thing to safeguard the future of civilization, I asked finally, what should that one thing be?

I thought he'd plump for unleaded fuel, reading *Hamlet*, or joining the Citizens' Front for the Restoration of Public Morals. Instead he said, 'To slow down. The danger of a more instantaneously communicating world is that people can get pressured into making dangerously quick decisions. Try to arrange for your life to be less hurried. Contribute to a less hurried world, and get back in touch with the cycle of the seasons.'

Right. So if you want to give one in the eye to the likes of Oswald Spengler, start by switching off that mobile. Answer no questions without a week's notice. Go out for long autumn walks and watch the flowers wilt – not your culture. You heard the man: *slow down*.

Simon was checking his pager. 'Excuse me,' he said, 'I just have to warn my next appointment I'm going to be late...'

Homo Sapiens: the fossil record

So what's really going to happen? Will we climb inexorably upwards (the *Star Trek* scenario) to a state of interplanetary harmony, gadgetry and bliss? Or will we go the other way?

I'm not a prophet. I'm not even a good guesser. On the other hand, I am wired up for e-mail, and – as everyone knows – out there in the dimensionless ether of cyberspace some very strange things can happen. It didn't surprise me, therefore, to find stuff blowing into my mailbox from the far-distant future – stuff in which was buried the following anonymous transcript. I reproduce it as given:

WEBFOOT:	At this point I'd like to welcome Dr Bernie Gadzook from the Institute of Theoretical Geology. Dr Gadzook, we understand you have made a discovery that throws light on a recent mass extinction...
GADZOOK:	Well, if you call 55 million years ago recent, yes.
WEBFOOT:	Until now we thought this was caused by asteroid impact, is that right?

GADZOOK: Absolutely. But of course there's never been any direct evidence for it. With asteroid hits you expect to see large amounts of the heavy metal iridium in the geological record. There's no iridium here.

WEBFOOT: But you've found something else, right?

GADZOOK: Well, by comparing sites across the planet we've identified a complex assortment of deposits we call the *Grunge Layer.*

WEBFOOT: The Grunge Layer?

GADZOOK: It consists mainly of carbon dioxide, non-biodegradable polymers, and chip grease – and, every now and again, one of *these*. If we could see the picture now...

WEBFOOT: Good heavens!

GADZOOK: This one's a male. Straightened out, he'd have been almost six foot tall.

WEBFOOT: Only two eyes, though.

GADZOOK: Yes, and both pointing towards the front, which was a handicap. But look what's written on the shirt.

WEBFOOT: *OLAY, OLAY, OLAY, OLAY, WE ARE THE...*

GADZOOK: We think it says *CLAMPS.*

WEBFOOT: *Clamps?* What does that mean?

GADZOOK: Frankly it's mystifying. Our guess is these creatures belonged to some kind of weird cult.

WEBFOOT: And you think the Clamps were instrumental in causing this mass extinction?

GADZOOK: Well, Clamp-like remains are most plentiful where the Grunge Layer is thickest. We'll have to do more work before we can prove the connection.

WEBFOOT: Any ideas?

GADZOOK: Quite often life forms like this acquire what we call 'bad survival habits' – patterns of behaviour that

	produce short-term gratification but long-term disaster. Once that happens they're goners from the word go.
WEBFOOT:	So you wouldn't rank the Clamps as intelligent, strictly speaking?
GADZOOK:	Put it this way, any species that drowns in its own chip grease could use an evolutionary audit.

11

And Then...?

Assistant District Attorney Mike Freeman pulls his Buick onto a dusty verge and we climb out. 'That's it,' he says, pointing.

A couple of hundred yards away I can see some pyramids of rubble and a bullet-riddled white bus. An American flag hangs upside down on the retaining fence. We're looking at the remains of the Branch Davidian compound in Waco, Texas, a couple of months after leader David Koresh has brought his followers to a suicidal showdown with the federal authorities.

The place should be a war grave. In fact, it has turned into an impromptu souvenir market. Outside the locked gates is a man called Bill Powers, a time-management trainer turned T-shirt vendor, his goods neatly laid out on packing cases. One of them reads: *Mount Carmel, Where the Cows Know How to Throw One Heck of a Barbecue.* Another offers terms for site purchase: *Must sell due to slight fire damage. If interested, we'll throw in at no additional charge one million rounds of ammunition and two M-1 tanks, slightly used, low mileage.*

Bill had been in Waco visiting his sister when the shooting began. Anyone else would have taken cover. Bill watched it all from a nearby hilltop, then phoned up an artist and printer. By 3 o'clock next morning he'd produced 300 T-shirts to sell to the arriving media. Retelling the story, he's almost beside himself with glee.

'They put me on every front page of every major newspaper in the whole United States,' he grins. 'I was on CNN, *48 Hours, Good Morning, America*. I was selling between 500 and 800 shirts a day, at $16 a pop.'

At that kind of multiple, $16 a pop can make you a lot of money. Overall so far he's grossed $300,000 dollars – enough to buy a brand-new van in cash and set up a lucrative sideline in clothes retailing under the unlikely name *Have-T-shirts-Will-Ship*.

It's hard not to like him. And even if you suspect his grandmother might be on the inventory list, you have to admire his nose for the quick buck. To Bill Powers, Doomsday as espoused by the Branch Davidian Sect seems to mean almost nothing at all. He's a man standing – literally standing – with his back to tragedy. There it is behind him, the remains of a world ending, and he's wringing your hand and asking you to buy the T-shirt.

How to get it on with the Master of Living Slack

There are other, less blatantly commercial ways of doing what Bill does. For instance, if you don't actually want the world to end, but still can't get enough of frenzied end-time revivalism, you might just consider joining the Church of the SubGenius.[1]

Founded in Texas in 1978, this spoof cult has attracted around 100,000 members, many of them brought in through a perky internet site. Its central and completely fictitious figure is the pipe-clenching J. R. 'Bob'® Dodds, end-time prophet and Master of Living Slack. *Slack*? Well, it's hard to explain, but *slack* is the attitude-type-thing you need if you want to help cult leaders Reverend Stang, Pastor Nekkid and St Janor Hyper-cleats combat 'the Conspiracy to silence the weird and

TIMES of HEAVEN   *Classifieds*

miscellaneous

Dull, unadventurous and pessimistic soul, 5'6", more Boris Karloff than Robert Redford, hates music, travel, theatre and dining out, seeks similar for possibly very long-lasting relationship. No slim, sincere, warm-hearted, easygoing, attractive, lively, confident and unpretentious types who like wine and riverside walks. Serious inquiries only. Voicemail #4699.

HAD TOO MUCH OF A GOOD THING?
Meet old friends on a weekend break to the **OTHER PLACE**.
Cruises on the Styx.
Hot-tubs en suite.
Choose from our famous selection of curries.

$69 (return)
INFERNAL TOURS
For Your Holiday From Hell

JUDGEMENT COMING?????
For full legal representation contact Intercessor Associates, the top specialists in Soul Litigation. 0002-89556-1459872656798. All cases on a No-Win-No-Hope basis.

---

immaculate ♥ CONNECTION

HEAVEN'S PREMIER INTERNET SERVICE PROVIDER.
5 MILLION YEARS FREE ONLINE

NOW SHOWING at New Jerusalem's only multi-screen cinema complex. Cinema 1: BAMBI (U), 3.00, 5.00, 8.30. Cinema 2: Gian di Patmosini's REVELATION: THE MOVIE (U), Friday 5.00 – Monday 4.30 (bring sleeping bags). Cinema 3: LAST TANGO IN PARIS (U) (edited version), every fifteen minutes from 2.00 to 11.00. Popcorn 50p (Milk & Honey flavour only).

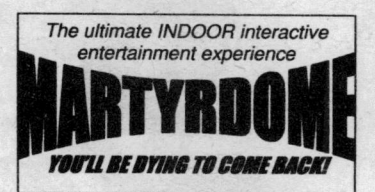

The ultimate INDOOR interactive entertainment experience
MARTYRDOME
YOU'LL BE DYING TO COME BACK!

Almighty, Omniscient, Omnipresent. Consubstantial, Co-eternal Deity, N/S, Creative Type with GSOH, loves jazz, needs a bit of light relief. You know where to find Me. Discretion appreciated. No religion PLEASE.

'Bob'®, Prophet of Slack, worshipped (and marketed) by the Church of the SubGenius. J. R. 'Bob' Dobbs is a registered trademark of the SubGenius Foundation Inc. and is used here with permission.

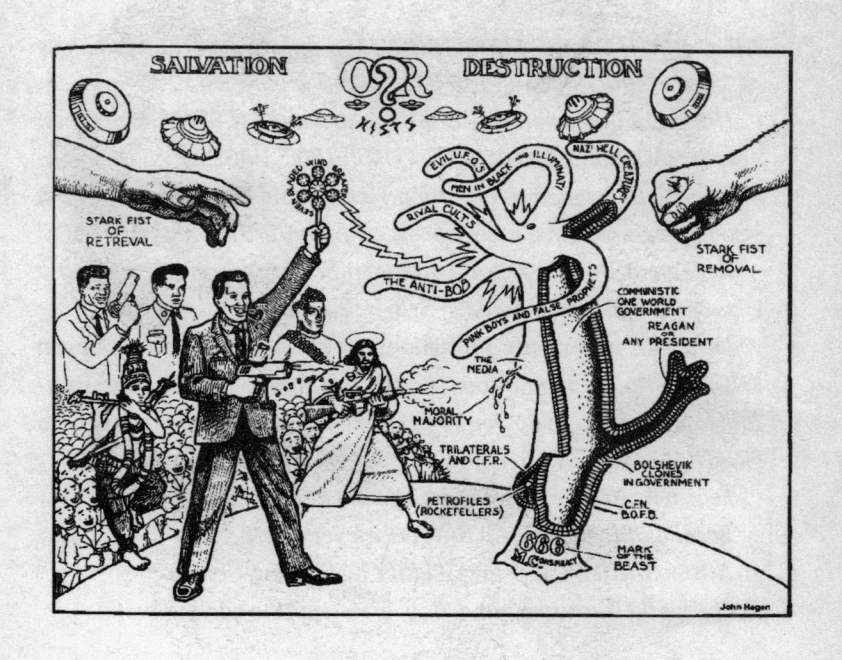

The religious universe at seen by the Church of the SubGenius.

abnormal'. For one dollar they will ordain you. Meanwhile, there is no problem known to man (or woman, or for that matter tuna fish or bottled prunes) that 'Bob'® can't sort out:

> THE CHURCH OF THE SUBGENIUS – the only 'faith' that promises ACTION – THRILLS – SUCCESS IN SEX AND BUSINESS!
> Using SubGenius secrets of BULLDADA and MOREALISM you can now MIRACULOUSLY ELIMINATE COMPULSIVE URGES such as smoking, eating, sleeping, working; end baldness, constipation, sex-money problems, assouliness, and painful shortage of SLACK!
> Become a Doktor of the Forbidden Sciences ... make religion a kick-ass adventure! Indulge in Self-Help through Raising Hell!
> 'Bob' is a way of life to millions – yet half of them don't even KNOW it! He is the one true LIVING SLACK MASTER with the spiritual know-how to help you BASH THROUGH the locked doorway to FINANCIAL HEAVEN. He is the only real Short-Cut to Slack.
> Fear THE STARK FIST OF REMOVAL no longer!
> Become PHYSICALLY ATTRACTIVE – overnight!
> Attain STATUS-LUCK-PROSPERITY by blowing them off!
> The world is a turkey, and 'Bob' gives you the carving knife!

The cult confidently predicted Doomsday on 5 July 1998. By all accounts, the accompanying party was quite a blow-out. The world didn't end – no one expected it to – and after some orchestrated wallowing in self-parody, the Church of the SubGenius resumed its cheerfully inane onslaught against the forces of oppression. Next Doomsday: 5 July 1999.

Significantly, turning the end of the world into an annual damnationfest hasn't hit their membership roll. On the contrary, they claim, 'We tripled last year's attendance with yet crueler and more barbaric tests of Faith.' Church of England, take note.

— AND THEN...? —

In their different ways, both Bill Powers and the SubGenius cult cock a snook at the idea of universal doom. To use a turgid phrase, they both *affirm life* – and why not? After all, life deserves to be affirmed. While there's beer to drink and moonlit skies to smooch under, why bother with abstractions like the end of time? Well, no reason at all, perhaps – except that life has a supply-side deficiency. It's not a renewable resource. Beginnings imply endings; Big Bangs bounce back into Big Crunches; to be alive is to know, absolutely and without hope, that one day you're going to be dead. You may not see the skies open or the hordes converge on Armageddon, but like it or not, your own personal world will have an end. Sooner or later the game will be over. The screen will go blank. And then – what?

Marilyn Agee would tell us that we zip to Saturn. Matthew Dumbrell would say that we arrive at Liverpool Street in the New Jerusalem for our rendezvous with Ron. By contrast, sinewy old rationalists like Bertrand Russell will insist that we die and rot. And the rest of us, strung out somewhere between these extremes, are tempted to leave the *AFTERLIFE* box blank and skip to the next question. The very word *afterlife* seems like a contradiction in terms. You're not exactly dead. You're not exactly alive. So what *are* you?

I cast around for advice.

Heaven: jobs for life vs the morgasm

It may surprise you to know that Jehovah's Witnesses don't believe in heaven. No fluffy clouds and harps for them. The afterlife begins right here on earth.

'That's why we're interested in environmental issues,' Paul Gillies told me. 'The Bible gives vivid descriptions of that new order. It talks about abundance of food for all. About people dwelling in security. It talks about peace between mankind and animalkind. About people building their own houses and having occupancy. It really talks about getting rid of all the divisive elements that we've got today. It's quality of life as it was meant to be.'

But what, I asked, would people *do* for all that time? Would there be work? Clearly for the 144,000 saints whose job is to 'rule as kings' there's a role in the cosmic civil service. But what about everyone else?

'Oh yes,' said Mr Gillies. 'Adam and Eve were meant to develop the planet. So there's much work to be done in caring for the environment. And there's lots of other projects you could get interested in. Science is only beginning to tap many areas of interest. With time on your hands and with abilities, there's no end to the sorts of industry you could get involved in.'

'And there's no time limit on that.'

'It goes on forever.'

So: anything you like, from microprocessing to heavy chemicals – and make sure you've got a *very* detailed career plan. But what happens when you get home at night? I asked Mr Gillies whether there would be – for instance – sex in heaven. The question seemed to catch him off guard.

'Well, we expect so,' he said, 'because we expect the family arrangement to go on. So who knows what God's eventual purpose will be? The Bible talks about populating earth until it's full. You have to have sex between a man and a woman who are properly married to have that.'

Cosmo's Mandi Norwood was less interested in heavenly employment prospects. Sex, however, is a subject she holds forth on with a passion Billy Graham reserves for the salvation of souls. Naturally there will be sex in heaven. But, I asked, did she think it would be *better*?

'Oh, I don't think it could *possibly* be any better,' she replied. 'I mean, there is heaven on earth, isn't there? And women, particularly,

AND THEN...?

are so confident about their own sexuality now, and so in control. When you have that kind of control, it doesn't *get* any better.'

Seeing me raise an eyebrow at this, she grinned and went on, 'Also, we've just invented the *morgasm*.'

'The...?'

'In the next issue of *Cosmo*. It tells you how to climax again and again and again. There are a lot of different orgasms. For example, you've got the 10-second, 10-minute and 10-hour orgasm. So it would be lovely to have a 10-hourer, and then just have a little snooze on your cloud while the man of your dreams strokes your foot.'

'For a hundred years.'

'That *is* heaven.'

That wasn't how the Jehovah's Witnesses put it. And yet in one way these two images of heaven – the heavy industry and the decimalized-orgasm-plus-foot-stroking – are chiselled from the same stone. I asked Mandi if she'd read Julian Barnes' *A History of the World in 10½ Chapters*,[2] where the writer dreams of waking up in heaven and finding that everything is just as he'd always wished it would be, right down to Leicester City football team winning the English FA Cup.

What Barnes' character experiences in his first week more or less sums up his entire experience of heaven: 'I played golf and had sex and met famous people and didn't feel bad once.' After a few thousand years he's done everything in every possible way. He can get around the golf course in 18 shots. He's not only played in the Leicester City's cup final but *scored the winning goal*. He's had sex with almost everyone. And yet it's slowly dawned on him that, 'After a while getting what you want all the time is very close to not getting what you want all the time.' And he's beginning to see why, even in this most ideal of ideal worlds, everyone sooner or later takes up the option to *die off*.

I don't think Mandi Norwood plays golf. But she was definitely into the meeting famous people. 'I would just love to talk to Audrey

Hepburn. And Marilyn Monroe. And I'd like to find Freddie Mercury and tell him how fab his last concert was.' I put it to her that (heaven forfend) one can take only so much of Freddie Mercury, and that, like the character in Barnes' book, she might eventually find heaven – even her heaven – a teeny bit repetitive. But she wasn't going to give up that easily. 'Oh, I don't know,' she said. 'I could wallow around in a department store like Harvey Nichols for ever and a day. That's my other idea of heaven.'

And then...

With respect, I'm not quite convinced. In essence such views of heaven aren't much different from the one I got from an elderly lady of my father's acquaintance. I'd asked her what she thought would happen after she died. 'Ooh,' she replied, with what appeared to be a surge of ecstasy, 'there will be daily evangelistic crusades, with Jesus himself as the speaker!'

Even then, I have to say, the idea of heaven as a never-ending church service didn't much appeal to me. But it didn't appeal because to see heaven as unlimited indulgence of your particular earthly joy is to make it something other than heaven. Human experience doesn't offer us enough Lego to construct the heavenly palaces. You need more bits. Different bits. Bits that no one's invented yet. Heaven is meaningless if it's a creation of our own minds – a place where we all wind up sitting on our rucksacks saying, *been there, seen this, done that.*

The point is underlined by the Bishop of London. Feeling I should consult at least one official minister of religion, I'd chosen the least stuffy bishop I could think of, and gone to meet him at the Old Deanery by St Paul's. If you're used to the kind of twittering clergy

AND THEN...?

wheeled on in television drama, Richard Chartres comes as a bit of a shock.

'If one were starting to give pictures of heaven,' he boomed, 'with our suspicious modern minds and our extensive information, we could immediately discern what the roots of those pictures were. That great witty canon of St Paul's, Sidney Smith, when asked for his vision of heaven, said it was eating pâté de foie gras to the sound of trumpets. It was obvious he'd overdosed on Guild Hall banquets. So you see very quickly where the furniture comes from, and that kind of furniture no longer conveys conviction. You have a situation where cynics sit before bishops and say, "Come on then, you convince me, give me your picture of heaven," and the bishops start floundering and talking about love and that sort of thing, and it's totally unconvincing.'

More than unconvincing: it's funny. The sheer mundanity of the heavens we believe in – their dully familiar clang – finally makes them comic. Which, of course, is a good reason for writing a book about them. But it's not the only reason. In one way the prophets of universal doom are right: sooner or later our individual worlds all end. Somewhere on the calendar ahead there's a day with my name on it, and a day with yours, and this fact both fascinates and frightens us. We're no longer certain what dying means. We casually say death is the end – the click at the end of the tape. But the thought brings little comfort, and in practice we quietly agree to talk about other things. Better not to have our journey of life spoiled by reminders that we're not going anywhere.

In the end, then – if you'll forgive the pun – Doomsday poses a question we can evade but not avoid. We laugh at the wacky end of end-time belief because it's wonderful, bizarre and funny. But we have to decide for ourselves what awaits us. I have my own answers, but I won't start in on those now. From here on, it's over to you.

Appendix I

Revelation: the Summary

In the court of heaven the seven-horned, seven-eyed Lamb is declared worthy to open the scroll of seven seals.

The four horsemen of the Apocalypse emerge, variously coloured. The last one, Death, has Hades on his heels, and is given permission to lay waste a quarter of the earth.

At the fifth seal, the souls of the martyrs under the altar demand to know how long it will be before God judges the earth. They're given new clothes and told to wait a bit.

The sixth seal: earthquake; sun turns black as sackcloth made of goat hair; moon turns to blood; the stars fall. The sky is rolled up. Everyone on earth runs for cover.

The angel from the east calls for time-out while the 144,000 servants from the great tribulation have God's seal placed on their foreheads.

Seventh seal opened. Heaven is silent. On earth, thunder and earthquakes continue as an angel hurls down a censer of prayers.

Seven angels with trumpets prepare to blow.

At the first four blasts a third of the following things are destroyed: vegetation (in a hail of fire and blood); sea creatures and ships (by a fiery mountain that falls into the sea and turns it to blood); drinking water (by the star Wormwood that falls on a third of the rivers and springs). Also lost: a third of the sun, a third of the moon, a third of the stars, and a third of the day and night.

Interlude as passing eagle calls woe to the inhabitants of the earth.

At the fifth trumpet blast a falling star opens the Abyss, from which pour world-darkening smoke and a horde of armoured locusts with women's hair and scorpions' tails. Under their king Abaddon (Greek: Apollyon) they subject mankind to five months of deathless torture.

APPENDIX I

The sixth trumpet sounds. Four angels bound at the great river Euphrates are released in the form of 200 million mounted troops, who kill a third of mankind with plagues of fire, smoke and sulphur.

Ignoring these warnings, the survivors persist in worshipping demons and refuse to repent of murder, sexual immorality and theft.

An angel with a rainbow on his head announces the seventh trumpet.

Two witnesses wearing only sackcloth arrive in the holy city after the Gentiles have trampled it for 42 months. They prophesy (1,260 days) and are then killed by the Beast from the Abyss. Their bodies lie (3.5 days) gloated over on the streets of the great city called Sodom and Egypt. But then they come back to life and are taken up to heaven in a cloud. A severe earthquake brings down a tenth of the city and kills 7,000.

The seventh trumpet is blown.

A woman clothed with the sun gives birth to a son who will rule the earth with an iron sceptre. An enormous red dragon with seven heads and ten horns tries to eat him, but God snatches the woman up and puts her in a safe house in the desert.

A heavenly war breaks out. Michael plus angels vs dragon plus angels. Michael wins. The dragon is thrown down to the earth, where he furiously resumes his pursuit of the woman. Eluded, he goes off to wage war on her other children, those who obey God's commandments, teaming up with a ten-horned, seven-headed Beast from the sea who was wounded with the sword and yet lived. This Beast mesmerizes the world for 42 months, and is then joined by a second (two-horned, lamblike) Beast who acts as the first Beast's representative. No one can buy or sell without the Beast's name on his right hand or forehead. The number of the name is 666.

Now made up to their full complement of 144,000, the martyrs 'who did not defile themselves with women' are found standing with the Lamb on Mount Zion. A flying angel announces God's impending

DOOMSDAY

judgement. The earth is harvested, and the gathered grapes are thrown into the winepress of God's wrath. The blood flowing from the press rises to the height of a horse's bridle for a distance of 180 miles.

Now seven angels in linen and golden sashes pour out the seven bowls of God's wrath.

People with the mark of the Beast break out in sores. The sea clots like a dead man's blood, killing all sea creatures. The rivers are turned to blood and the sun given power to scorch people with fire. Then the Beast's kingdom is plunged into darkness. The waters of the Euphrates dry up.

Though they gnaw their tongues in agony, men still refuse to repent.

Jumping like frogs from the mouths of the dragon, Beast and false prophet, three unclean spirits go out and gather the kings of the earth for battle at Armageddon.

The seventh bowl produces the mother of all earthquakes. The great city is split into three, other cities razed. Islands and mountains disappear. Hundred-pound hailstones rain down from the sky. The great prostitute ('Babylon the Great'), who sits on many waters ('peoples, multitudes, nations and languages') and who was drunk with the blood of the saints, is finally destroyed. Deprived of their customers, the merchants wail.

Riding on a white horse and with a sword protruding from his mouth, the Word of God leads the armies of heaven into battle against the Beast and the kings of the earth. The Beast and the false prophet who represented him are thrown alive into the fiery lake of burning sulphur, while the rest are put to the sword and become birdfood. The dragon – the Devil, or Satan – is locked in the Abyss for a thousand years.

In the first resurrection the martyrs come back to life to reign with Christ. A thousand years later Satan is released from his prison and goes to Gog and Magog – the four corners of the earth – to gather

APPENDIX I

them for battle. But no sooner have they surrounded God's city than fire from heaven devours them. Satan is finally thrown into the lake of burning sulphur along with the Beast and false prophet. The dead are called up from earth, sea and Hades to stand before the great white throne, and everyone whose name is not written in the book of life is consigned to the lake of fire.

With the war trials over, the New Jerusalem descends from heaven, and we all move in.

Appendix II

The All-time Funniest Gag

And you thought I'd forgotten. Well, you have no idea what dedication it takes to troop around public houses all day buying people drinks and recording jokes. Nor can you guess what a drag it is transcribing them. Anyway, out of the 38 days, 4 hours, 51 minutes and 10 seconds of joke I've waded through, there is – in my humble, unsolicited, but correct opinion – just one that passes the test. More people have got more laughs out of this joke than from any other gag on the face of the earth. Believe it. Would I tell you a lie?

在上歷史堂時 , 老師問 :「你們誰知道中國誰最先有英國名字 ?」
一位同學立即回答 :「詩聖杜甫 , 他的名字叫子美 , 出生在一千年前 .」
另一位同學立即回答說 :「不 !應是孔子 , 他的名字叫仲尼 , 出生于二千五百年前 .」

Notes

Chapter 2

1 It was widely accepted, for instance, that God had mandated the westward expansion of the United States. In the *United States Magazine and Democratic Review* (July–August 1845), John L. O'Sullivan prophesied 'the fulfillment of our manifest destiny to overspread the continent allotted by Providence...'

2 Yes, it's true. Anyone interested in purchasing a Rapture Ruler can find details at: http://home.coqui.net/lastcent/rrtract.html

Chapter 3

1 See: http://www.erols.com/rlogston/endtimes/index.htm

2 From Peter and Paul Lalonde ('Your tour guides to the future') at This Week in Bible Prophecy. See: http://www.twibp.com/interviews/teachers/lindsey/lindsey.076.html (Part1).

3 Rapture Ready, home of Todd Strandberg, 'the prophecy pack rat', can be found at http://www.novia.net/`todd

4 See Rapture Ready, as above, main page.

Chapter 4

1 This and the following description taken from Bernard McGinn, 'Portraying Antichrist in the Middle Ages', in *The Use and Abuse of Eschatology in the Middle Ages*, edited by Werner Verbeke, Daniel Verhelst and Andries Welkenhuysen (Leuven: Leuven University Press, 1988), pp. 1–48. Thanks to INFORM at the London School of Economics for tracking that one down.

Chapter 5

1 Antichrist Bob's site can be found at: http://bennyhills.fortunecity.com/fawlty/370

2 Receive thou the Mark of the Beast – official web-site of the Antichrist. See: http://www.nyct.net/~ao
3 See E. W. Bullinger, *Number in Scripture: Its Supernatural Design and Spiritual Significance* (London: Samuel Bagster & Sons Ltd, 1976).
4 *Great Joy in the Great Tribulation: Simplified Prophecy for the Last Days*. Publicity for the book is on site: http://gvtc.com/~jsearcy
5 Chris J. Beard: Beast of the Sea. At: http://www.docsa.com/greatjoy/chris.html
6 There is a broad-based resistance movement now active on the net. For further information visit: http.jihad.net
7 Originator of the argument unknown.
8 Footnote from my daughter: Barney is a wonderful, harmless, educational TV personality, and Daddy should get off his case.

Chapter 7

1 Edited from *Conspiracy Currents*, No. 29: http://www.conspire.com/curren29.html
2 Diana Tumminia and R. George Kirkpatrick, 'Unarius: Emergent aspects of an American flying saucer group', in James R. Lewis (ed.), *The Gods Have Landed: New Religions From Other Worlds* (New York: State University of New York Press, 1995), pp.89–90. This version of the Unarius story is based on Tumminia's and Kirkpatrick's account.
3 See Peter Worsley (ed.), *The Trumpet Shall Sound* (London: Paladin, 1970).
4 Von Daniken's position as summarized by John Allan in *The Gospel According to Science Fiction: God Was an Ancient Astronaut, Wasn't He?* (Libertyville, Illinois: Quill Publications, 1976), p. 22.
5 See: http://members.aol.com/phylata/conc.html

The article on which this section draws comes from a collection copyright © 1993, 1994, 1995, 1996 by J. R. Mooneyham. 'This article may be freely copied and distributed in paper and electronic form without charge if this copyright paragraph and link to J. R.'s WebFLUX Page are included.'

Chapter 9

1. Leon Festinger, et al., *When Prophecy Fails* (Minneapolis: University of Minnesota Press, 1956).
2. Leon Festinger, et al., ibid., pp. 187–188.
3. See 'Flying-saucer folk left godless' in *Independent*, 26 March 1998.
4. These details from Ted Daniels, PhD, director of the Millenium Watch Institute. Information on the Institute and its work can be found at: http://www.channel1.com/mpr/mpr.html
5. *The Time is at Hand*, p. ii (Foreword).
6. ibid., p. 101.
7. Quoted in Raymond Franz, *Crisis of Conscience* (Atlanta: Commentary Press, 1992, 2nd edition), p. 199.
8. The total of 416,167 converted in three years after 1975 suggests there was more to this rise than apocalyptic fever. That, however, wasn't apparent beforehand.
9. Quoted in Raymond Franz, op.cit., p. 200.
10. *The Watchtower*, 1 May 1968.
11. *Kingdom Ministry*, May 1974.
12. *The Watchtower*, 15 July 1976.
13. *The Watchtower*, 15 March 1980.
14. As reported by *FAIR News*, Autumn/Winter 1995/6, p.10.
15. *The Watchtower*, 15 March 1980.

Chapter 11
1 See http://www.subgenius.com
2 Julian Barnes, *A History of the World in 10½ Chapters* (London: Jonathan Cape, 1989), pp. 283–309.